Salvatore Canals
JESUS AS FRIEND

Salvatore Canals was born in Madrid in 1920. He joined Opus Dei when still a student and went to Italy in 1942, where he spent the rest of his life. He was ordained priest in 1948. From 1957 to 1965 he was joint editor of *Studi Cattolici*. He was an auditor of the Roman Rota and a consultor to the Congregation for the Clergy, the Congregation for the Sacraments, and the Pontifical Commission for the Means of Social Communication. He suffered ill health during the last years of his life, but even during that time his faith and serenity were evident; he died on May 14, 1975.

Jesus As Friend is probably his best book; it has gone into numerous editions, particularly in Spanish translation. This is the fourth English edition, the first one published by Scepter.

JESUS AS FRIEND

SALVATORE CANALS

SCEPTER PUBLISHERS

Nihil obstat: Stephen J. Greene, censor deputatus.
Imprimi potest: Dermot Archbishop of Dublin, June 22, 1979.
The *Nihil obstat* and *Imprimi potest* are a declaration that a book or publication is considered to be free from doctrinal or moral error. This declaration does not imply approval of, or agreement with, the contents, opinions, or statements expressed.

Original edition *Ascetica meditata* (Edizioni Ares: Milano) © 1981
Translation © Michael Adams 1986

Reprinted by Scepter Publishers, Inc., with the permission of Four Courts Press, Dublin, Ireland.

ISBN 978-1-88933-403-5
This edition © 1997 Scepter Publishers, Inc.
www.scepterpublishers.org
info@scepterpublishers.org
212-354-0670

Third printing 2018

Printed in the United States of America

CONTENTS

Preface   vii

Jesus As Friend   1
Our Christian Vocation   5
An Ideal for Life   8
Interior Life   11
A Heart Guarded   15
The Main Road   18
Christian Hope   21
Humility   27
Meekness   30
Humiliations   34
The Road of Pride   38
Celibacy and Chastity   41
True and False Virtues   45
Serenity   48
Criticism   52
Temptations   56
Imagination   60
Examination of Conscience   64
In Our Father's Presence   67
The Bread of Life   70
I Will Be with You Always   73
Death and Life   76
Fraternal Correction   80
The Danger of Good Things   85
The Weeds and the Good Wheat   89
Light from Bethlehem   94

PREFACE

I wanted to write this preface earlier, for the first edition, but my publisher's deadline barely gave me time to put these articles in order.

They were originally commissioned by *Studi Cattolici* [an Italian journal of pastoral theology]. I had no intention of writing a book: they were simply a series of meditations, not arranged in any particular sequence, and I produced them with no great difficulty, for I was borrowing what I wrote.

To people like myself who sought his advice on the interior life, Monsignor Escrivá de Balaguer, the founder of Opus Dei, often used to say that in his ministry as a priest he used "only one 'pot'," only one teaching, which was valid for everyone—that holiness should be sought in the context of one's everyday occupations. Each of us had a right to dip his spoon into this "pot" and help himself to whatever he needed, in his particular situation, to get nourishment. I, for one, did that time and time again; and later on I put pen to paper, turning my meditation into this book.

My purpose in writing was simply to comment on some of the teachings of Monsignor Escrivá. Really his contribution was much greater than mine: I had dipped so often into that "pot" that my commentary often amounted to no more than enlarging on something he said, paraphrasing him or even literally transcribing his way of putting things. You know what I mean: I was like a child in a toy shop who cannot make up his mind but wants to take everything, were he allowed.

I first met the founder of Opus Dei in 1940. It is difficult to explain all that meeting meant for me. Later on, in Rome, I was able to get to know him very well. He spoke always with great conviction, and he derived his energy from a strong interior life that was wrapped in an extraordinary naturalness; he set one on fire with divine fire. I have meditated on his teachings countless times and asked God to make them my very life, to help me learn to sanctify everything I do. I pray now that those who read these meditations may learn the same lesson.

As you read *Jesus As Friend* and some phrase enkindles in you the same fire, be in no doubt: the man to thank is Monsignor Escrivá, for he is the principal author of the thoughts you find in this book.

S. C.

JESUS AS FRIEND

Try to see that from their early youth or from adolescence they are inspired by an ideal—to seek Christ, to find Christ, to become Christ's friend, to follow Christ, to love Christ, to stay with Christ.

JOSEMARÍA ESCRIVÁ DE BALAGUER, OCTOBER 24, 1942

IN THIS HANDFUL of clay that we consist of—which you and I *are*—there is, we know, an immortal soul that tends toward God; and it desires God with all its strength, even when it denies him. This tendency toward God, this overpowering desire, this deep nostalgia, God himself wanted us to concentrate on the person of Christ, who lived on this earth as a man of flesh and blood, like you and me. God wants this love of ours to be love for God made man, whom we know and whom we understand, because he is one of us. He wanted it to be love for Jesus Christ, who is forever alive: there is his lovable face, his loving heart, the wounds in his hands and feet, and his open side. "Jesus Christ is the same yesterday and today and for ever" (Heb 13: 8).

Well, this same Jesus, who is perfect God and perfect man, who is way, truth, and life, who is the light of the world and the bread of life, can be our friend if you and I so wish. Listen to Saint Augustine, he speaks from the experience of an incisive mind and a great heart: "I can be God's friend if I so wish." But to achieve this friendship you and I must approach Jesus and get to know him and love him. Friendship with Jesus helps us make great progress; with him we shall find happiness and tranquility. We shall have sure standards to tell us always how we should behave; we shall be going toward our Father's house; and we shall, each of us, be another Christ, for that is why Jesus Christ became man: God became man so that man might become God.

Yet there are very many people who forget about Christ, or who do not know him or do not want to know him, who do not pray in Jesus' name, who do not pronounce the only name by which we can be saved, and who look on Jesus Christ as a figure in history, or as a faded glory, and forget that he came and lived "so that all should have life and have it more abundantly" (Jn 10: 10). Note that all these are people who want to reduce Christ's religion to a set of rules, to a series of penal edicts and onerous duties. They are souls suffering from a remarkable short-sightedness, seeing in religion only something tiresome, burdensome, and depressing. Theirs are cramped and lopsided minds that look at Christianity as if it were a calculating machine; theirs are mean, disillusioned hearts that know nothing of the riches of Christ's heart; false Christians who try to remove Christ's smile from the face of Christian life. To them, to all these people, I would say: "Come and see" (Jn 1: 46). "Taste and see that the Lord is good" (Ps 33: 8).

The news the angels brought to the shepherds on Christmas night was a message of joy: "I bring you good news of great joy which will come to all the people: for to you is born this day in the city of David a Savior, who is Christ the Lord" (Lk 2: 10-11). The hope of the nations, the Redeemer, he whom the prophets had announced, the Christ, God's Anointed, was born in David's city. He is our peace and our joy; and on his account we invoke our Lady, Mary the Mother of Christ, as "cause of our joy."

Jesus Christ is God, perfect God. Let us, then, you and I, express our adoration to him in these words, which the Father placed on Peter's lips: "You are the Christ, the Son of the living God" (Mt 16: 16). And let us also repeat Martha's confession or that of the centurion or the man born blind.

But Jesus Christ is also a man, a perfect man. Savor that title which he loved so much: the Son of man, as he called himself. Listen to Pilate: "Behold the man!" (Jn 19: 5), and turn to look on Christ. How near we feel to him now, my friend: Christ is the new Adam, but we feel him to be even closer to us than that. For the gift of immunity to pain meant that Adam could not suffer, whereas you, Lord, suffered and died for us: you are indeed, Jesus, perfect man, the perfect man. When we try to imagine the perfect type of man, the ideal man, even without wanting to, we think of you. And at the same time, good Jesus, you are Emmanuel, "God with us."

And all this holds true forever. That body which he assumed, he will never set aside. Be hungry and thirsty to know the holy humanity of Christ and to live very close to him. Jesus Christ is a man, a real man like us, with body and soul, intelligence and will, like you and me. Remind yourself of this often: it will make it easier for you to approach him in prayer or in the Eucharist, and your life of piety will find in him its true center, and your Christianity will be more authentic.

Intimacy with Jesus. To know, love, imitate, and serve Jesus, you have to approach him confidently. "You cannot love what you do not know." People get to know each other thanks to a warm, sincere, intimate, and steady relationship. But where are we to seek the Lord? How can we approach him and get to know him? In the Gospel, thinking about him, contemplating him, loving him, following him. Through spiritual reading, studying and getting a better grasp of the science of God. Through the blessed Eucharist, adoring it, receiving it.

The Gospel, my friend, should be your book for meditation, the focus of your contemplation, the light of your soul, the friend of your solitude, your *vade mecum*. Accustom your eyes to contemplate Jesus as perfect man, who cried when Lazarus died and over the city of Jerusalem; let them see Jesus suffer hunger and thirst. Get used to finding Jesus sitting at Jacob's well, tired after his journey, waiting for the Samaritan woman. Consider the sadness he felt in the Garden of Olives: "My soul is very sorrowful, even to death" (Mt 26: 28), and the way he gave himself up to the tree of the cross, and the nights he spent in prayer, and the energy with which he threw the dealers out of the temple, and the authority with which he taught. Become full of confidence when you see him—his heart moved by compassion for the crowd—multiplying the bread and the fish and giving her son back to the widow of Naim and restoring Lazarus to the affection of his sisters. . . .

Go to Jesus; approach him in the silence and concentrated work of his hidden life, in the difficulties of his public life, in his passion and death, in his glorious resurrection.

Each of us finds in Jesus the exemplary cause, the model of the holiness made to his measure. If we cultivate his friendship we shall get to know him. And in the intimacy of our confidence with him we shall listen to his words: "I have given you an example, that you also should do as I have done to you" (Jn 13: 15).

Before we finish, look confidently at the blessed Virgin. For she, better than anyone else, knew how to carry Christ's life in her heart and contemplate it within her: "Mary kept all these things, pondering in her heart" (Lk 2: 19). Ask her to help you; she is Christ's Mother and yours, and we always go to Jesus through Mary.

OUR CHRISTIAN VOCATION

How clear it was, to those who knew the way to read the Gospel, that everyone was called to holiness in ordinary life, in one's work, staying where one was! And yet for centuries the majority of Christians did not grasp this—the ascetical phenomenon of many people seeking holiness in this way, without leaving their place, sanctifying their everyday occupation and sanctifying themselves in it: this just didn't happen. And very soon, by dint of its not being practiced, the doctrine was forgotten about and theological reflection became absorbed in the study of other ascetical phenomena, reflecting other aspects of the Gospel.

JOSEMARÍA ESCRIVÁ DE BALAGUER, JANUARY 9, 1932

I WAS SPEAKING the other day to a young man, in just the same way as I'm speaking to you now. I was trying to convince him of the need to live in a Christian way, frequenting the sacraments, being a soul of prayer, and giving all his actions and his whole life a supernatural focus. Jesus, I told him, needs souls who, with great naturalness and a generous self-surrender, live an integral Christian life in an everyday setting. But in his eyes you could see his soul was resisting, and when he spoke he tried to find excuses because he just did not want to accept the ideas I was putting before him. A few minutes later he summed it all up very sincerely (perhaps he had never even put it to himself before): "I cannot live the way you say, because I am very ambitious." And I remember that I replied, "Look, here in front of you is someone much more ambitious, a man who wants to be a saint. For my ambition is so great that nothing on earth will content it: I am ambitious for Jesus Christ, who is God, and for Paradise, and for eternal life."

Let me now continue that conversation here. Don't you think that all of us Christians should have a holy ambition of this kind? The Christian vocation is a vocation to holiness. All Christians, simply because they are Christians—and never mind what position they occupy, what they work at, or where they are—have a duty to love God above all things: "You shall love the Lord God with all your heart, with all your mind, with your whole soul and with all your strength" (Lk 10: 27). But this simple, clear idea, which is the first commandment and sums up all God's law, has lost its force; today it has little effect on the lives of many of Christ's disciples.

Lord, how impoverished the Christian ideal has become in the lives of your people. They seem to think, Jesus, that the ideal of holiness is too far above them and that not all Christian hearts can aspire to it. I have heard it so often; holiness—that's something for priests to aim at and for those whom a special vocation has led to a cloistered life. We men of the world are quite happy if we live an unpretentious, unexaggerated Christian life; we humbly forego those flights of soul even if it means that now and then we get a vague sense of sterility and pessimism. Holiness (many people say to themselves, out of prejudice and ignorance) is not for us: it would be presumptuous, arrogant, unbalanced, inappropriate, fanatical for us to seek it. So they surrender before the battle is begun.

I would like to shout out at many Christians: "*Agnosce, christiane, dignitatem tuam:* Christian, recognize your dignity." Listen to me, my friend: set yourself free of preconceived ideas, and let your mind open out, serenely. The Christian vocation is a vocation to holiness. Christians—all of us without any exception—are, in Saint Peter's phrase, "a chosen race, a royal priesthood, a consecrated nation, a people set apart" (1 Pet 2: 9). The first Christians, who were aware of their dignity, referred to each other as saints.

When, my friend, are you going to lose your fear of holiness? When are you going to convince yourself that our Lord wants you to be a saint? Whatever your circumstances, whatever your job is, no matter what age you are or your physical condition, independent of your activities and your social position, if you are a Christian, our Lord wants you to be holy, to be a saint.

"Be perfect, as your heavenly father is perfect" (Mt 5: 48). Jesus addressed these words to everyone; to each he proposed the same goal. There are different ways, because there are many different mansions in the Father's house; but the goal, the aim, is one and the same for all Christians—holiness.

That is why, after two thousand years of Christianity, we Christians should really be of one mind and heart in this aim for holiness, just like the first Christians: "And the multitude of the believers were of one heart and of one mind" (Acts 43: 32). This firm, luminous conviction is supported by those words that Saint Paul addressed to all the faithful: "This is the will of God, your sanctification" (1 Thess 4: 3). On so many grounds are you asked and required to be holy—baptism, which made us children of God and heirs to his glory; confirmation, which made us Christ's soldiers; the holy Eucharist, in which our Lord himself gives himself to us; the sacrament of penance; and marriage, if you have received it. All those are so many callings to holiness. Heed them.

Once our prejudices have been shed and our mind enlightened by a new light, it is easy to formulate our resolutions—to make the problem of holiness a very concrete and very personal problem, to make it "our" problem. God our Lord—we are intimately, deeply convinced about this—wants us to be saints because we are Christians.

Let's raise our eyes, our hearts, and our wills to God. Savor the things on high, seek the things on high (cf. Col 3: 1): our Christian dignity opens up before us limitless, serene horizons. Let us take a deep breath of the fresh air that comes from those distant lands; it renews our youth, just as Scripture says the eagle's youth is renewed (Ps 102: 5).

Let us once and for all recognize the emptiness of our miserable ideas and detest them. Let us deplore the time we have wasted and dismiss our silly fears. We are no longer afraid of holiness, and we now, at last, recognize that our hearts, as the Psalmist put it, took fright too often when there was no reason for fear.

Let us commend ourselves to our Lady, the Queen of all saints and the seat of wisdom, to have the idea of holiness become ever clearer, stronger, and more concrete in our lives.

AN IDEAL FOR LIFE

. . . this ordinary, everyday, unassuming life can be a way to holiness: you do not have to leave your place in the world to seek God, unless the Lord has given you a religious vocation; all the ways of the earth can be opportunities for an encounter with Christ.

JOSEMARÍA ESCRIVÁ DE BALAGUER, MARCH 24, 1930

IF YOU WILL allow me, I shall now keep on thinking about the same subject. I feel the time has come to give thanks humbly to God; as the Psalmist says, "the snare is broken and we have escaped." The bonds of prejudice, preconceived ideas, mistaken notions have been untied, and we are now convinced that holiness has to open up a way in our minds and in the minds of all Christians.

We have set out along that way: the pearl of great price has been shining in front of us; that hidden treasure has brought joy to our hearts. However, I have known souls, many souls, who have reached this point and then, for one reason or another (you can always find "reasons" and excuses), have gone no farther. It is sad, isn't it; and yet we can learn from it. They were souls who *had* seen but then closed their eyes or fell asleep; souls who had begun but did not continue; people who could have done a great deal but did nothing.

What we have to do is to move from idea to conviction and from conviction to decision. We have to become very deeply convinced that holiness is something for us; that holiness, more than anything else, is what the Lord is asking us for. "Only one thing is necessary" (Lk 10: 24). I hope that you will always keep a firm hold on these divine words: the only defeat that can be conceived in a Christian life—in your life—consists in dawdling on the road toward holiness, ceasing to aim at the goal. My friend, life and the world would lose their meaning were it not for God and souls. This life of ours would not be worth living were it not continually lit up by an eager and loving search for God.

Listen: "What does it profit a man if he gains the whole world but loses his soul?" (Mt 16: 26). Why think about so many things, if we then forget the only one that counts? What is the point of solving all our problems if we don't solve the most important one? What value have our achievements, our successes (our "getting to the top") in life, in society, in our work, if then we get shipwrecked on our way to holiness, to eternal life? What kind of profit is it, what is your business worth, if you suffer loss of Paradise and fail in the business of your holiness? What is the purpose of your studies and your skills, if you are ignorant of the meaning of life and of knowledge of God? Your pleasures: are they enjoyable if they deprive you forever of the enjoyment of God? If you do not really, ardently seek holiness, then you possess nothing. "Seek first the kingdom of God and his justice, and all the rest will be added on to you" (Mt 6: 33).

Please meditate on these ideas, and gather others of your own: think about your own life, today, as it is; reflect on your present position and on the dangers threatening your soul. This will help strengthen your deep conviction that you should get nearer to holiness, for that is the only way to happiness on earth and happiness in heaven.

"My Lord and my God!" (Jn 20: 28). We should put all the decision and resolution of these words of Saint Thomas into our effort and look for holiness above anything else. You should be firmly decided to be a saint and to press ahead, no matter what it costs. What wonderful example Saint Teresa gives us. She goes forward on her way, challenging tiredness and misgivings and weakness and death: "even though I am exhausted, even though I cannot go another foot, even though I burst, even though I die."

And do not forget that what holds us up on our way is not the difficulties and obstacles (which really do exist); what holds us up is our indecisiveness. "It is not that we fail to dare because things are impossible: things are impossible because we do not dare." Indecisiveness is the only real obstacle; once we overcome it, there is no other—or, rather, we can easily deal with the other obstacles we meet. May our "yes" to God be a firm "yes," and with his grace may it be ever bolder and more absolute.

Lacordaire said that "eloquence is the daughter of passion; give me a man with a great passion and I will turn him into a great orator for you." I might say: Give me a committed man, a man who feels a passion for holiness, and I will give you a saint. May no one surpass us in our desire for holiness. Let us learn, with God's help, to be men and women of strong desires, to seek holiness with the full force of our conviction and with our whole heart: "as the deer yearns for the waters of the cool springs" (Ps 41: 2).

If you, my friend, who are reading these lines, are young, think about your youth; youth is the time for generosity. What use are you making of it? Do you know how to be generous? Do you know how to make it produce a fruitful and effective search for holiness? Do you know how to set yourself on fire with these great ideas . . . how to convince yourself . . . how to commit yourself? But if you have already set out on life, don't worry, because God's time for you is now. All times are good times for him, and he calls us at all times (at the third hour, at the sixth, and at the ninth) to become convinced and make our minds up and desire holiness—as Jesus taught us in the parable of the workers in the vineyard.

It doesn't matter what age you are; it doesn't matter what your position is or what your circumstances are or who you are: you have to convince yourself, commit yourself, and desire holiness. You well know that holiness does not consist in extraordinary graces received in prayer, or unbearable mortification and penance; nor is it the inheritance only of those who live in lonely oases, far from the world. Holiness consists in faithful and loving fulfillment of one's duties, in joyful and humble acceptance of God's will, in union with him in your everyday work, in knowing how to fuse religion and life into a fruitful and harmonious unity, and in all sorts of other ordinary little things you know so well.

This path seems . . . The path is simple and clear. Convince yourself, decide, desire! Make your effort and your struggle specific, and persevere with love and faith. Our blessed Lady, Queen of all saints—if you ask her for light and protection—she will give you support and consolation in the struggle.

INTERIOR LIFE

We have need of a rich interior life—a sure sign of friendship with God and an essential condition for any kind of work with souls.

JOSEMARÍA ESCRIVÁ DE BALAGUER, MAY 31, 1943

WITH HIS FINE mind Saint Thomas Aquinas saw that all the values of this world simply disappear if compared with the least of supernatural values; and he expressed this idea in a metaphysical way, when he said: "*Bonum unius gratiae maius est quam bonum naturae totius universi:* A single grace is a greater good than all the natural good of the entire universe." A contemporary writer, also imbued with this great notion, has expressed it in another way: God our Lord—he has said—is more concerned with a heart in which he can reign, than with the natural government of the entire physical universe or the government of all the empires of the world. Well, today I wish to talk to you about this kingdom of God, where the Lord finds his delight; that kingdom of God which is within us; that kingdom of God which is as wonderful as it is unknown.

The heart of man is like a cradle in which Jesus is born again; and that is why, in all hearts that have chosen to receive him, Jesus himself—although in different ways—grows in age, in strength, and in grace. Jesus is not the same in everyone, but according to a person's capacity to receive him he shows himself as a child, or as an adolescent in full development, or as a mature man. Christ's desire is to reign: to be born and to grow in the heart and in the life of Christians. In this way, he wants to make each Christian—you, me—another Christ. And we should all respond to this calling of grace, to this invitation from Jesus, repeating the words of the Precursor: "He must become more and more, I must become less and less" (Jn 3: 30).

This transformation in Jesus Christ, this union with God, which is the result of interior life, affects everything we do and makes us feel and enjoy the consoling parable of the vine and the branches. "I am the vine and you are the branches. He who remains in me, and I in him, bears much fruit; for without me you can do nothing" (Jn 15: 5).

Be a branch united to the vine, a soul of deep interior life. Don't delay in recognizing that your thoughts will be transformed by the wisdom that supernatural life brings; it will cause you to think with God's thoughts and see the world and life with God's eyes. If you have this union with Jesus Christ, you will no longer have a pagan mind. You will not merit that reproach from Christ: "Do not the pagans do as much?" (Mt 5: 47). Your outlook on the world, deeply supernatural, will give light and warmth to your words. Your supernatural spirit will also transform your affections. You will understand Saint Paul when he says, "Have in your hearts the very sentiments of Christ Jesus" (Phil 2: 5). For Jesus' sentiments, full of purity and understanding, full of love for souls and compassion for those who have strayed from their path, are the patrimony of those who have been transformed in Christ. Through this union of thought and of sentiment with Jesus Christ, through this renewal of your intellectual and emotional life, your interior life will penetrate all your external activity. Your actions, the flowers and fruits of your interior life, will be full of God and will reveal the superabundance of your love for him. Only then will they be truly "deeds rich in God's presence."

Your union with Jesus has to be, above all, interior. For your thoughts, desires, and affections are the most delicate and most intimate part of your life, and they are also the most generous and most precious part of your holocaust. And all this interior world—this pulsating world of your heart—is precisely what the Lord is asking of you. If you give the Lord only your external acts but deny him or measure out to him only a bit of the most intimate part of your life—your desires, your affections, your thoughts—you will never be an interior soul.

Do you want to check to see whether you are a soul of interior life? Ask yourself this question: Where do I usually live in my thoughts, affections, and desires? If your thoughts, affections, and desires all converge on Jesus Christ, it is a sure proof that you are an interior soul. But if they lead you far away from God, it is a sign, and also a sure sign, that you are not a soul of interior life. You should not forget that "where your treasure is, there lies your heart" (Mt 6: 21). And the only treasure of souls with interior life is Jesus, that Jesus—they add—"whom I saw, whom I loved, in whom I believed, whom I preferred above all else."

So you can see, my friend, that the great battlefield of souls who aspire to a genuine, deep interior life is the heart. God's battles are won and lost in the heart. That is why the "guard of the heart" is the basic rule of the ascetical life. When souls love and do not hinder God's work, he leads them to real union with him and sets up his kingdom within them, a kingdom of justice, of love, and of peace.

If these considerations have opened your eyes to the fact that the kingdom of God is completely interior—"the kingdom of God is within you" (Lk 17: 21)—you should now open your eyes to a new truth. You should remember that "the kingdom of heaven is taken by force" (Mt 11: 12); the way leading to this interior kingdom is a way of mortification and of purification.

Now that you feel you are a branch united to the vine, now that you want to be increasingly more like that, you must listen again to what Jesus says: "I am the true vine, and my Father is the vinedresser. Every branch of mine that bears no fruit, he takes away, and every branch that does bear fruit, he prunes that it may bear more fruit" (Jn 15: 1–2). For you to yield more fruit, to consolidate your union with the Lord, you need pruning, purification. Don't be afraid of the pruning knife: "My Father is the vinedresser." For by means of this pruning the Lord will purify your mind and your will, your heart and your memory. You cannot go forward one step in the life of union with God without taking another step on the path of purification. And to do that you need to cooperate with the Lord: when the moment comes for pruning, let it be done. And when you see shoots and leaves fall, be happy: think of the new fruit that this pruning promises soon to produce.

The abundance of these fruits depends on your interior life, on your degree of union with God. "He who abides in me, and I in him, he will yield much fruit" (Jn 15: 5). May your external activity, your intense action, not lead you away from God.

Listen once again to the Lord: "Abide in me." Remember that the interior life is the soul of the apostolate. The greater your union with God, the more fruit your apostolate will produce. (Of course, we are talking about your fruit and not about success, which is something completely different.) A man of interior life is more effective with a few spontaneous words than a person who is not very interior but who gives a marvellous intellectual dissertation.

I want to remind you, too, that the apostle's sensitivity to the problems and needs of his apostolate does not depend on the degree he is immersed in external activity, or on his cleverness and efficiency, but on his degree of union with God.

Before finishing this short conversation with our Lord, let us listen once more to the words of Jesus: "Abide in me."

A HEART GUARDED

We have to teach everyone that it is a wonderful thing to be a Christian,
because a believer's soul is God's temple, where the Blessed Trinity dwells;
we must also tell them that if they want to attain Christian perfection
they must put up a bold fight in the struggle of the interior life, because
the kingdom of God is taken only by force.

JOSEMARÍA ESCRIVÁ DE BALAGUER, FEBRUARY 2, 1945

I ASK YOU to listen to that great saint of the Church, Augustine,
acknowledging the happy experience of his heart and his clear
mind: "You made us, Lord, for yourself, and our heart is restless
until it rests in you." This saint, I am sure you know, looked
everywhere to quench his thirst for truth and love. After many
sad experiences his great and noble soul let out the cry I have
just transcribed; it is a genuine confession. This brilliant and
generous man was looking for happiness and peace; his search
was in vain until he found everything when he found God.

All of us experience this restlessness, and we need to quell it.
Until he does quell this restlessness, until he fills this emptiness, a
man's heart yearns, suffers, and searches. Every man's life is the
story of a pilgrim, a man making his way in search of happiness.
Everyone—some consciously and others (the majority) uncon-
sciously—is looking for God.

And, so, people can be divided into two kinds—those who
love God with their whole heart, because they have found him;
and those who seek him with all their heart, because they have
not yet found him. To the former the Lord has given the commandment: "You shall love the Lord your God with your whole
heart" (Mt 22: 38); to the latter he has promised: "Seek and you
shall find" (Mt 7: 7). Ask yourself to which of these groups you
belong, and then you will know what you must do. Don't forget
that if you see or feel that you need something, what in fact you
need is God our Lord, who is not yet present in your life or who
is not yet there enough.

I would like to remind you of a very simple truth, a truth

basic to everything we have been considering. Man's heart, everyone's heart, even the heart of the soul dedicated to God, has been created for happiness and not for mortification, for possession and not for renunciation. And this need for happiness and for possession is something wonderful; it is a real need, *now*; it is something beautiful, which expresses itself now, before we enter into Paradise. If the human heart has been created for happiness—a happiness that begins here below, on earth, and is to be found only in God—you have to admit that the path to it can be none other than "the guard of the heart."

The science of custody of the heart consists in planning and struggle, defense and attack, knowledge and decision, renunciation and suffering; but all this aims at happiness and its possession. Guarding the heart means keeping it for God, living in such a way that our heart might become the place where he reigns, that it might contain all the loves compatible with our state in life, but might be based harmoniously on the love of God and be ordained to it. Guarding the heart also means loving purely and passionately those whom we ought to love, while excluding jealousy, envy, and restlessness, which are sure sources of disorder in love. Guarding the heart means, always, maintaining an order in our love. The science of guarding the heart teaches the Christian to go deep into his soul to discover its tendencies.

How few people look sincerely at this fruitful and hidden source of human life, the heart! How much evil and how much greatness live and vibrate in the reaches of the human heart! My friend, if we take a good look at our heart, we will not be long in discovering that God, human nature, and the devil are the three eternal combatants in that spiritual struggle which takes place there each day. And we will also understand that God's battles are lost or won in the heart.

In this way we will understand the depth of the reproach made by Jesus to the Pharisees: "These people honor me with their lips, but their hearts are far from me" (Mt 15: 8). Our Lord, who loves the clean of heart and who wants to set up his throne in our hearts, cannot accept this hypocritical and formal service.

A soul accustomed to guarding the heart recognizes that most of his actions are either exclusively natural or are a mixture of nature and grace. He recognizes only too well how seldom his actions derive entirely from grace, how seldom they are perfectly supernatural. For the supernatural character of an action is continually threatened on all sides—at the outset, in its execution, and at the end.

That is why those souls turn the custody of the heart into a continuous watchfulness over their own intimacy, into an alertness in all their actions at the very moment of carrying them out. If we imagine the heart to be a battleground, we can say that this science shows us how to live continuously as sentinels in the vanguard of the army.

True, the way is not easy; but when the heart has reached complete purification, God our Lord, by his presence and love, takes over the soul and its powers—memory, intelligence, and will. And in this way purity of heart leads man to union with God, a union to which other routes do not normally lead.

Once someone has achieved purity of heart, he can easily practice all the virtues he needs; and he will possess the spirit or the "essence" of all those other virtues he gets no opportunity to practice; and that is what God our Lord desires.

In the school of the heart we can learn, in an instant, more than we could be taught by all the teachers of the world in a hundred years. Without the guard of the heart, we will never reach holiness. Without the guard of the heart, we will never reach holiness however much we try; on the other hand, with it and without other external actions, many souls have been sanctified. And that is also the way that leads to happiness, to that peaceful and complete rest of the heart in God.

THE MAIN ROAD

If we have in our souls the same sentiments as Christ had on the cross, we will be able to turn our whole life into continuous atonement, a constant prayer and permanent sacrifice for all mankind: the Lord will give you a supernatural instinct for purifying all your actions, raising them to the level of grace and turning them into means of apostolate.
JOSEMARÍA ESCRIVÁ DE BALAGUER, FEBRUARY 2, 1945

SHOWING a very justifiable concern, a spiritual writer has asked whether it is really right nowadays to insist *"exclusively"* on that effort to achieve human perfection which Christianity implies if it is practiced in a serious and self-sacrificed way. Taking up this cry of alarm, I wish to suggest to you, my friend, that perhaps the most characteristic feature of the world today is its lack of "theological outlook."

Here you are, alone with God, to think about things in his presence; to reflect on your personal experience, on your relations with other people, on their reactions to things (and your own), on their activities (and yours), on their attitudes to spiritual values and to the testing experiences of life and to so many events affecting the Church and giving rise to problems that can endanger the good of souls. Don't you think that many Christians (and maybe you too) forget about the greatness of God and of his Church? Isn't it true that a theological outlook on things is being pushed out of many minds? Doesn't it seem from the way Christians behave and speak that the "sense of the cross," which has such an intimate connection with theological outlook, is even despised?

You and I know very well that to see God you have to die: "No man has ever seen God" (Jn 1: 18). The same sort of thing happens in our interior life. To see Jesus and to get to know him in the luminous darkness of faith, to live on ever more intimate terms with him, we have to learn to die to ourselves. We need this "theological outlook," this "sense of the cross": *ubi crux ibi Christus*, where the cross is, there is Christ.

Jesus himself told us a secret: "The kingdom of God is within you" (Lk 17: 21); and he showed us a way when he added: "The kingdom of heaven is taken by force" (Mt 11: 12). If we don't have this "theological outlook," this "sense of the cross," our life runs the risk of being merely human: we stop living as Christians and change to living as pagans—at best, as good pagans.

The cross is our only hope. Set up the cross, Christ's cross. Set it up in your mind, so you can understand its value and how necessary it is. It will help you avoid being pagan in your judgments and deliberations. Set it up in your will, so you can love it and accept it, not with resignation but with love. Set it up in your actions: it will help them share in the redemptive efficacy of the cross. Holiness is achieved on the cross, because the cross means the death of sin, and sin is the only enemy of holiness. Let us listen to our Lord's voice: "If anyone wishes to come after me, let him deny himself, take up his cross daily and follow me" (Lk 9: 23). For a Christian there is no other way: his is the king's highway, the main road of the holy cross, on which everyone has a right to travel.

This cross, Christ's cross, the holy cross, we should take up—so we can walk carrying it—"daily." The day we do not feel on our back the weight of the cross, the day our mind fails to recognize its value: that is the day when we do not live as disciples of Christ. You should look at the cross with faith and carry it with love. Never feel yourself, not even for a minute, a "victim." The cross does not make victims; it makes saints. It does not cause sad faces but happy smiles. A person who lives in this way understands that there is only one victim—Jesus Christ, who suffered and died for all of us, who suffered and died abandoned.

When we Christians—you and I—carry the cross, it makes us happy; we discover the one and only true happiness, which is sharing in God's happiness. But if we want to carry the cross, which makes us his disciples "daily," we have to go looking for it. And this has to be our first resolution—to open our soul's eyes, the eyes of faith, to open them wide, so as to discover the cross of Christ in our lives.

What then will the cross be for us? Look: what do you find most difficult in your everyday life? Well, that is the Redeemer's cross for you. Those tough temptations you meet, your ill health, your heavy, demanding work, the defects of the people among whom you live, who hurt you . . . Have a supernatural outlook! All this, for you, is the cross of Christ. Make a firm resolution to recognize it and embrace it when you catch sight of it as you make your way. Ask our Lord to show you the mystery of the cross, and you will take huge steps on the way to holiness.

And now that you know what Christ's cross is, now that you appreciate its value and how much you need it, how easy it is to carry! Carry it joyfully, lovingly. Carry it generously, and you will learn to hide it from those around you as you would hide a treasure. Hide it behind a generous smile, and you will discover, in the depths of your soul, what our Lord's words mean when he says, "My yoke is easy and my burden is light" (Mt 11: 30)—for he, the good Cyrenean of souls, will help you carry it.

And don't just carry your own cross: carry your brothers' crosses as well. But above all, show them the value of the cross; pray the Lord on their behalf to help them love the cross that lies in their concern or their anguish, the cross that lies in whatever causes them pain.

The cross, and only the holy cross, will make your life as an apostle effective and fruitful. "When I am lifted up from the earth, I shall draw all men to myself" (Jn 12: 32); when I can lovingly, like Jesus Christ, be on the cross, then I will draw to you, Lord, all the souls around me: then will I truly be a co-redeemer with Christ.

And do not forget that the blessed Virgin Mary, the Queen of martyrs, is also Queen of peace. Approach her confidently; keep her company, at the foot of the cross.

CHRISTIAN HOPE

. . . we are not alone, for God exists, and he has called me into exist-ence: he supports my being and strengthens me. Moreover, he has chosen me with special love, and, if I trust him, he will grant me constancy and strength to follow my way, for once he begins something, he finishes it: he always brings things to perfection.

JOSEMARÍA ESCRIVÁ DE BALAGUER, SEPTEMBER 29, 1957

AMONG THE VIRTUES that leave the deepest impression on the human spirit, which in the clearest of ways influence the life and activity of men, is the Christian theological virtue of hope. In other words, if you take the same man and see him living in the fresh air of hope or lying under the weight of despair, what you see is a giant or a pygmy—and you are right. In our relationships and contact with others, we are every day witnesses—and it causes us surprise and pain—of these amazing changes; for, per-haps our own century more than any other suffers from a short-age of this virtue. How many philosophies, how many attitudes, how many moods of people nowadays have their roots in souls without hope, people who cannot decide between opting for anguish or for fear, an anguish that nothing can dispel, a fear that nothing an alleviate.

The truth of the matter is that man cannot live without hope. Hope is a calling from the Creator, who is the beginning and end of our life; it is a calling that no man can escape; it is the voice of the Redeemer, who ardently desires the salvation of all men ("who wants all men to be saved"—1 Tim 2: 4). No one, without losing his peace of soul, can refuse to listen to this voice; it is the deep nostalgia for God, which he himself has left in us—as a wonderful gift—through bringing about, for each one of us, those ineffable "works of his hands," which, in the language of the theologians, are called Creation, Elevation, and Redemption. Few in Christian history have been better able to express this deep nostalgia in the human heart, with the conviction of knowledge acquired by experience, than Saint

Augustine. He was a writer with sharp intuition and great insight, and in one cry from his great soul he was able to define the whole condition of man, a wayfarer on this earth: "You made us, Lord, for yourself, and our hearts are restless until they rest in you."

Let us stay with these words for a moment to try to shed some light on our worries and to help explain our anxieties. The nostalgia each one of us bears in his heart cannot be escaped; it is rooted in our very person, which is destined one day to see God and to enjoy him forever. This nostalgia will be with us always; it will be our companion as we make our way, the friend of the happy parts and the sad parts of our every day on earth. Yet it can be and ought to be relieved, and that in fact is what the virtue of hope is for. The second part of Saint Augustine's phrase is really a release valve: ". . . until they rest in you." If this valve were blocked, our restlessness and nostalgia would turn into despair and anguish.

As long as we are on the road, as long as we are wayfarers on this earth, we carry with us this nostalgia for God and a dark restlessness growing out of our uncertainty about achieving our final goal (for no one, unless he has a private revelation from God, can feel certain about his own eternal salvation); this nostalgia and uneasiness can be—and indeed ought to be (we are now convinced of it)—relieved by Christian hope. We Christians in this world are supported by hope; and when hope, together with faith, falls away at the end of our life on earth, then we will have the joy of forever possessing God and the joy of the kingdom of charity, where there will be no fear, no sense of risk of any kind. At the end of our human comings and goings, each of us will have either the joy of possession or the despair of seeing himself forever deprived of God.

Hope, a theological virtue, makes us continually tend toward God, relying, for reaching him, on the help he has promised us: "Be of good heart, I have overcome the world" (Jn 16: 33). The formal motive (as the theologians usually put it) of this virtue is God, who always helps us: *Deus auxilians*, God our help, the almighty aid. However, sometimes it happens that we Christians (this is one of a whole string of contradictions in our life) replace this great and beautiful virtue with human hopes, which are smaller, though they may be beautiful. It's not that Christians should not have human hopes and aspirations; on the contrary: we can say that there are beautiful, noble hopes that have more right to be in our heart than in any other. But also here—in the "province" of hope—we have to have in our soul and in our heart the proper order, a hierarchy and harmony of hopes, and no human hope—however noble and beautiful it is—should obscure the light and lessen the strength of our hope of possessing and enjoying forever, in eternal life, God, who is our ultimate goal.

So it sometimes happens in our life that God, through his providence, demolishes some human hope that our personal scale of values had perhaps prized too highly. In this case his purpose is to prevent anything taking over that position in our heart which only the great hope for God should fill. What we must do then is follow the way Providence leads us and learn to reestablish the right order of values in our scale of hope. God will give us real help to calm those human hopes that, in deference to the order established by him, we have not hesitated to put in their proper place. If, on the contrary, in reaction to God's spoiling our human hopes, we were to reply by stubbornly pushing away our great hope of God, we would be digging with our own hands a pit of rebellion and despair.

I need not tell you, my friend, how many crises of that kind I have known; you too, in your experience, must have known many. Often we only see the human aspect of these crises, and we call them complexes or neuroses, when really they are something else and their diagnosis should be deeper and more spiritual.

One thing is certain: until we possess and practice the true Christian virtue of hope, our life will lack solidity and we will live in a situation of instability. We will move very, very easily into presumption, when everything is going well and our life is going ahead without hitches or disappointments, and we will swing to despair, which will settle down in our soul, the moment anything happens against our expectations, rubbing us the wrong way or upsetting our plans. If we really practice the virtue of hope, we become very resilient and live a trusting abandonment, in constant faithfulness to duty, which puts us precisely above this kind of fluctuation. Do you remember Christ's words to the threatening waters of the Sea of Galilee? "Be quiet, be still" (Mk 4: 32). They seem to represent the voice of hope, which imposes silence on the rumblings of discouragement. "And," the Gospel goes on, "there came a great calm." That is exactly the result hope produces—calm, serenity, peace.

Hope, theologians teach us, gives certainty of being on the right path; Saint Thomas says that hope tends with certainty toward its end. Despite our failures, our contradictions, and our faults, we should always hope in God; he has promised his help to those who ask it humbly and with trusting perseverance: "Ask and you shall receive" (Mt 7: 7). What shall we receive? Temporal goods, on certain conditions—that is to say, to the extent they are useful for our eternal salvation; the graces we need, with no conditions attached to them; and not only grace, but the Holy Spirit, *altissimum donum Dei:* the highest of all of God's gifts. And here we remember spontaneously what Jesus said to the Samaritan woman: "If you knew the gift of God . . ." (Jn 4: 10). If we truly knew and completely understood the gift of God, we would invoke the Holy Spirit much more often, and we would confidently ask him for everything we need to avoid straying from the right path and to reach our last end without falling or delaying.

We have to face this battle of Christian hope every day: "The Lord is my shepherd, there is nothing I shall want" (Ps 22: 1); we have to be fully aware (because this awareness forms part of the virtue of hope) that hope depends not on our merits or virtues but only on the mercy and omnipotence of God. In the light of hope, in other words, God more than ever appears "not as a weigher of merits but as the forgiver of our faults," as we pray in one of the prayers used in preparation for Communion. We have to base ourselves on the strengths that theological virtue brings us; in this way we learn to fight off tendencies to discouragement, which get in our daily way toward evangelical perfection. We should learn to resist—also every day—that gnawing pessimism which tends steadily to get worse with the exactions of time and the monotony of life. When we feel like that, we seem to remember two characters in the Gospel (they make an impression on us in a quiet and slightly melancholic sort of way)—the woman who was bent over and the man with the withered right hand. They betoken depression, tiredness, and inactivity: that is why they are particularly suitable for describing the effects produced in the human spirit by those moral diseases called pessimism and discouragement but really nothing other than the lack of the virtue of hope.

We must also make sure that pessimism and discouragement don't find their way into our apostolic life and weigh it down with barrenness. The Christian apostolate calls for constant strength, persevering tenacity, and unshakeable faith in the Lord's graces and in the mission he has entrusted to each particular man. To prevent any of the links in this chain from giving way, we need the strength that comes from Christian hope, which shows a man well tested in the apostolate how always to go back and start again at the beginning. The example of the apostle Peter is very useful to us—his doggedness at the time of the miraculous draught of fish. He ignores the fact that he has spent a whole night of useless effort ("We have labored all night and caught nothing"—Lk 5: 5); he says he is quite ready to start working again, in deference to what his Master says: "However, I will let down the net again in your name."

But not only should we try to get a grip on ourselves through the strength of Christian hope, we should be able to instill confidence and serenity in other people, opening the way to a really genuine apostolate of trust, after the example of the anonymous friends of the blind man whom Saint Mark tells us about; they encouraged him to respond to the Lord's call, with these beautiful words: "Be of good heart; get up, he is calling you" (Mk 10: 49).

Christian hope leads souls to abandonment: for a person who truly hopes in the Lord is always faithful to the will of God when he sees it clearly (a faithfulness that has to do with the virtue of obedience); in this way he is preparing his soul for abandonment to God's good pleasure. But this perfect abandonment, to which the virtue of hope leads us, is very different from "quietism"—as you very well know—for the simple reason that abandonment, when it is genuine, is accompanied by hope and by constant fidelity to our ordinary duties, even in the little things of every moment. Hope, in other words, makes demands on the Christian: it commits him, with all his strength and all his resources; it obliges him to keep going, to persevere on his path, even when all human supports have failed; in fact, it is then above all that true hope in God asserts itself in all its greatness. That is the moment for hoping in spite of everything ("in hope, he believed against hope," Saint Paul asserts of

Abraham); it is a moment that is particularly divine, a moment that God keeps for souls whom he especially loves.

Hope, my friend, should never be a comfortable substitute for laziness. Our Lord reminds us of this in two of his miracles—when he began to work miracles, in Cana of Galilee, changing water into wine, and when he multiplied the loaves and fishes in front of a huge crowd. In both miracles, our Lord's omnipotence took a hand when all human means had failed, when men had done everything they could do. The water was not changed into wine until the faithful servants filled the pitchers "up to the brim"; and before multiplying the loaves and fishes, our Lord asked for the total sacrifice of all their means of subsistence, that is to say, he asked for all the bread and fish they had; and he didn't mind that they had very little; what was important was that they should give him everything they had.

To practice the virtue of hope, nothing remains but for us to invoke the help of our heavenly Mother, who is our hope, my Mother in whom I trust.

HUMILITY

Truth, Saint Thomas says, lies in the understanding in so far as it is in agreement with the known object: and one could add that, if a man is not humble, he will find it difficult to know and accept the truth just as it is, in all its scope and with all it entails.

Josemaría Escrivá de Balaguer, October 24, 1965

I HAVE OFTEN thought—and I take this opportunity to write it down—that the virtue of humility resents its name and all that it implies. In other words, no other virtue is less valued and so little and so badly known; no other Christian virtue is so ignored and so deformed. The virtue of humility is a humiliated virtue. I cannot work out whether more harm is done it by people just forgetting about it and jeering at it or by the inaccurate and embarrassing way some people present it.

I feel that it is very, very necessary for us Christians to get to know this virtue better and have a real grasp of its importance, to strive to acquire it and practice it correctly. In this way we can show forth its true features to the eyes of a world suffering from vanity and pride. You and I ought to feel that Jesus Christ is inviting us to this effective and forgotten apostolate of good example when he says: "Learn from me, for I am meek and humble of heart" (Mt 11: 29). That's how our Lord wants us to be; he wants us to have that humility which is born in our heart and makes our actions fruitful. For the other humility, which is born and dies on our lips, is false: it is a caricature. Words, actions, and manners cannot in themselves create a virtue; but they can deform one. Our mind can open up for us the road of the heart and help us place there, to good effect, the seed of true humility, which, with time and God's grace, will put down deep roots and yield sweet fruits.

True humility begins at the bright point where the mind discovers and admits, sufficiently clearly for the heart to be able to love it, the simple, deep, basic truth that "without me you can do nothing" (Jn 15: 5). We ought to learn to break, with our proud hands, the white bread of evangelical truth and spread it out before our clouded eyes, which give so much importance to our ego and our qualities. Look, all our efforts to be better and to grow in love for Jesus and in the practice of the evangelical virtues will be in vain if his grace does not help us: "Unless the Lord builds the house, those who build it labor in vain" (Ps 126: 1). No amount of vigilance, no matter how attentive and constant it is, will be of any use without the strong and loving protection of his grace: "Unless the Lord guards the city, he watches in vain who guards it" (Ps 126: 1).

So, our words and our actions can do nothing if we rely on them to do good to souls. Our apostolate and our hard work, without the pure water of his grace, are merely sterile activism: "Neither he who plants nor he who waters is anything, but only God who gives the growth" (1 Cor 3: 7). But this grace—which is necessary for improving in virtue, for resisting temptations, and for making our apostolate fruitful—the Lord grants to those who are humble of heart: "God resists the proud and gives his grace to the humble" (1 Pet 5: 5).

The Lord, who, in his great goodness and with a watchfulness of refinement, gives his grace abundantly, does not use proud people to achieve his purpose: he is afraid they may condemn themselves. For, if he were to use them, they would discover in this grace (for this is how they act) an additional reason for pride, and for that vainglory they would incur additional punishment.

Humility, the saints teach us, is truth. What a fine reason that is for accepting it! "Help me to know myself, Lord" (Saint Augustine). This intimate and sincere self-knowledge will lead us by the hand to humility.

Let me tell you—for I have said the same thing to myself very often—that you are nothing: your existence you have received from God. You have nothing that you haven't received from him; your talents, your gifts of nature and grace, are precisely that—gifts; don't forget it. And grace is also a gift, deriving from the merits of our Savior. But to this nothing that you are, my friend, you have added sin, for you have often abused the grace of God, through malice or, at least, weakness. And to the two of these you have added a third, which is sadder still; in addition to consisting of nothing and sin, you have lived on vanity and pride. Nothing . . . , sin . . . , pride. What better foundation for our humility, for being really and truly humble, humble of heart!

The proud person and the unbelieving person have more in common than might appear. A person who is unbelieving is like a blind man who travels the world and sees created things without discovering God. A proud person discovers and sees God in nature, but fails to discover him and see him in his own self. If you discover God in yourself, you will be humble and you will attribute to him whatever good is in you: "What have you that you have not received?" (1 Cor 4: 7). You will not foolishly shut your eyes to any of the virtues or qualities that exist in your soul, for you know that they come from God and that one day he will ask you to account for them. You will strive to make them bear fruit; you will bury none of your talents. And while retaining the merit of your good works, you will know how to give God the glory of them: *Deo omnis gloria!* All the glory for God! Vain self-satisfaction will find no place in your humble soul.

Through the road opened by humility, God's peace will enter your soul. You have his promise: "Learn from me, for I am meek and humble of heart, and you will find rest for your souls" (Mt 11: 29). A heart that is sincere and prudently humble will never be upset by anything. Be sure, my friend, that, almost always, the cause of our ups and downs and of our restlessness lies in excessive concern over our self-esteem or a desire to be highly regarded by others. The humble soul puts self-esteem and others' regard into God's hands. And he knows that there they will be safe enough. So, get strength from humility to say to the Lord: If my self-esteem and the esteem of others are of no use to you, they are of no use to me either. And in this generous abandonment you will find the peace promised to the humble.

Let Mary's humility, my friend, be our consolation and our model.

MEEKNESS

Like the knight of La Mancha, they see giants where there are nothing but windmills; they become ill-humored, sour people, full of bitter jealousy, rough-mannered, finding fault with everyone, always looking on the black side of things—these people who are afraid of the rightful freedom of man, who do not know how to smile.

Josemaría Escrivá de Balaguer, June 16, 1933

My FRIEND, you who know the life of Jesus Christ are perfectly aware that our Lord chose to join meekness and humility on the same page of the Gospel. You remember his friendly, clear words: "Learn from me, for I am meek and humble of heart, and you will find rest for your souls" (Mt 11: 29).

Meekness and humility, you see, are two virtues that should always be in your heart, two sisters who live the same life, two precious metals that fuse together perfectly: one remarkable for its solidity, the other with a rare splendor. Two very positive and very virile aspects of our interior life, for by humility we win God's heart and by gentleness we attract and win over the hearts of our brothers.

Now that you are meditating in the presence of God, I want to tell you that this virtue is for everyone—so it is also for you. We all need it very much, because life is a continuous relationship with other people, a *convivenza,* a series of relationships, an opportunity for encounters of all kinds. Your family, your brothers, your friends, your social and professional relationships, your superiors, your peers, your subordinates: that is where the Lord is awaiting you. In all these *convivenze,* your Christian meekness should shine. If you are able to anoint your character with the strength of these virtues, your heart will become like Christ's: "I am meek and humble of heart."

A priest should be meek so that he can bring charity and Christian patience to his contact with souls, and in this way be effective; a Christian mother will ensure the strong, enduring education of her children if she is skilled in meekness; peace will reign in the family if this virtue is affirmed; and if meekness appeared in social and professional relationships, they would change considerably, and many who look in vain for peace elsewhere would not take long to find it.

We all tend to think that it is better and easier to do good by being noisy and bossy; that people can be taught by threats and pressure; that respect is obtained just by raising one's voice and being authoritarian. What room, then, is left in our life for Christian meekness? Why did Jesus recommend it to us in the Gospel?

How many times has life not replied to these questions by teaching us that effectiveness is hidden almost always behind the meekness of Christ—by telling us that goodness is the fruit gathered by those who seek and know how to find clear, friendly words, use them in a serene, persuasive way, and anoint them with the balm of good manners.

How often experience has taught us that corrections and reproaches, made without human meekness, have closed the heart of the person who should have received them. This should help us remember that, when we cease to be a father, brother, or friend to our neighbor, every word that leaves our lips carries the fatal germ of sterility.

Try always, through Christian meekness, which is friendly and affable, to hold the hearts of those whom divine providence has placed alongside you and given you to look after. For if you lose men's hearts, it will be difficult for you to bring light to their minds and get their wills to follow the path you show them.

My friend, you feel on your shoulders and in your heart responsibility for other souls, the weight of other lives: never forget that trust cannot be imposed; it must be inspired. And without the trust of the people around you, who work with you and serve you, how bitter your life will be and how fruitless your mission. A Christian mother will understand these words very well if she thinks about the education of her children; a priest, if he meditates on the welfare of the souls whom he and his cooperators are counseling; and an executive in an office or a factory will also understand them, if he stops to think about the welfare of his employees and associates.

Your ill-temper, your roughness, your unfriendliness, your rigidity (not very Christian!) are why you find yourself alone, in the loneliness of someone who is selfish, embittered, eternally discontented or resentful; and they are also why you are surrounded not by love but by indifference, coldness, resentment, and lack of trust.

With your good humor, your understanding, and your friendliness, with the meekness of Christ as part and parcel of your life, not only should you be happy but you should bring happiness to everyone around you, to the people you meet on the road of your life. As you go along, you should leave behind the good aroma of Christ (2 Cor 2: 15)—your constant smile, your serene calm, your good humor and your joy, your charity, and your understanding. You should become like Jesus, "who went about doing good" (Acts 10: 38).

Those who do not know the meekness of Christ leave behind them a cloud of discontent, a wake of animosity and bitterness, a trail of wounds that do not heal, a whole chorus of laments, and a string of hearts closed—for a while at least—to the action of grace and to trusting in the goodness of their fellow man.

Ask yourself, my friend, in a sincere, clear-sighted examination of conscience, what have you in fact left behind up to now? Those who have regarded you as a father, a brother, or a friend; those who have had contact with you as a superior or a colleague: what have they received from you? What has been the effect on their souls of having met you?

If you have seen your whole life in terms of apostolate, I must at least remind you of the promise Jesus made in one of the beatitudes: "Blessed are the meek, for they shall inherit the earth" (Mt 5: 4). Being gentle, being meek, means inheriting the earth, and that is the first condition for giving glory to God and bringing peace to men. If you and I, who want our lives to be completely taken up with the pursuit of goodness, do not know how to inherit the earth, attracting the hearts of men, how can we bring them to God? Before wanting to make saints out of all of those people we love, we have to make them happy and joyful, for nothing better prepares the soul for grace than joy.

You already know—I only want to remind you of it—that when you have in your hands the hearts of people whom you wish to improve, if you are able to attract them through the meekness of Christ, you have already gone half-way on your apostolic road. When they love you and trust you, when they are content, the field is ready for sowing, their hearts are open like fertile ground, ready to receive the white grain of your word as an apostle or educator. If you know how to speak without wounding, although you may have to correct or reprimand, hearts will not close themselves to you. The seed will fall on truly fertile ground, and the harvest will be plentiful. If things were otherwise your words would find, not an open heart, but a brick wall; your seed would not fall on fertile ground but "on the side of the road" of indifference or distrust, "or on the rocky ground" of a soul who is ill-disposed, or "among the thorns" of a wounded and resentful heart.

Let us never lose sight of the fact that our Lord has promised his effectiveness to friendly faces, cordiality, good manners, and clear, persuasive words that direct and form without wounding: "Blessed are the meek, for they shall inherit the earth." We should never forget that we are men relating to other men, even when we want to do good to souls. We are not angels—therefore our appearance, our smile, and our manners are factors that condition the effectiveness of our apostolate.

We cannot finish without asking Mary, sweet Mother, to look down in mercy on us: "Turn your eyes of mercy toward us." Under the gaze of so affectionate a Mother, we will understand very well the value and need and efficacy of Christian meekness.

HUMILIATIONS

God exalts in the very things in which he humbles. If the soul lets itself be led, if it obeys, if it totally accepts purification, if it lives by faith, it will see an unsuspected light, so wonderful that it will think it had previously been blind from birth.

JOSEMARÍA ESCRIVÁ DE BALAGUER, MARCH 24, 1931

IF PATIENCE IS the way that leads to peace, and study the way that leads to knowledge, humiliation is the only way to reach humility. Let us now, you and I, take that last consideration and pray about it, now that we are alone with God our Lord.

If we want to have a real, genuine spiritual life, we need to take humility seriously. And this concern for humility will bring us to ask ourselves how we should react, so as to get the best possible advantage for our spiritual life, to the humiliations the Lord makes us feel in the depth of our soul and causes us to meet in the course of our work.

There are moments—delicate moments—in the spiritual life, in which the soul feels deeply humiliated. Very specific, very clear illuminations from God our Lord uncover and emphasize how humiliating our wretchedness and our deficiencies, our inclinations and imperfections and defects, can be. The eyes of our soul are opened, and we see that we are something we don't want to be; we notice that we feel something we don't want to feel; we find that something attracts us in spite of the fact that we detest it. Many defects, which perhaps we were ignorant of up till then, appear, very clearly, very well defined; we are amazed. And the failures and deficiencies that our life has experienced storm their way into our consciousness.

At times of greater recollection, on days of retreat, for example, it is easy for our Lord to put souls on this road so they can grow in humility and get a deeper knowledge of themselves. At such times, in such circumstances, remember, my friend, the following words: "*Digitus Dei est hic:* The finger of God is here." Do not forget that it is God's love for you that is giving you this light of self-knowledge, this feeling of what you have been or what your are, this humiliation whose intensity has to push your soul along the road of humility. Do not forget that the Lord reserves this treatment for those whom he loves particularly: "Those I love, I reprove and chasten" (Rev 3: 19).

Therefore, my friend, our supernatural reaction to this humiliation should be an act of deep gratitude: "I thank you, Lord, for you have humbled me." That interior humiliation, that external failure, will leave your soul soaked in humility and will give greater holiness to your life—and very probably an unsuspected effectiveness to your activity.

But do not think that you are worse now that you can see something you did not see before, now that you feel deeply something you did not feel before, now that you have the opportunity to know some defect in your character, in your formation, or in your attitudes. You are not worse; or at least you are in the best position to set about being better. During those moments—if you make good use of them—you have already gone half way, for you now know where the evil lies that you should eliminate, you know the defect you should fight against, and you know what you should do to avoid being taken by surprise.

What, then, should our spiritual disposition and our supernatural reaction be toward these interior humiliations and these external factors that threaten the peace and tranquility of our interior life?

Our first reaction to all this must be one of humility—accepting the humiliation or the failure with true humility, with what is called humility of heart, because there it has its roots, and it is from the heart it gets all its strength. And not just accepting the humiliation, but loving it—loving our own wretchedness and thanking our Lord for letting us really know ourselves. As a consequence, we will avoid anything that is or might be a kind of interior rebellion against these humiliations or failures. What a lack of humility of heart we would show if we rebelled against this position of humiliation: the goodness and providence of God want to put us there so that we will mature and become more united to him.

Not only should you avoid rebelling in this way, but you should also try very carefully to avoid any kind of self-justification or offering of excuses to other people. If you are not truly humble, you will find lots of ways to justify yourself, to feed your pride. Your high idea of yourself will produce them with no difficulty; that is the sure way of nipping in the bud all the humility and effectiveness that God was reserving for your soul. Don't make excuses for yourself! Don't justify yourself to your soul when it is alone and humbled! Drown in humility that proud reasoning: it will only close up a wound that is healing badly. Have the courage to repel the counterattack of pride, which is trying to recover the ground your self-love has lost. Turn your back on the insidious caress of pride. Be convinced that this is the time to turn to God. Be happy to be misunderstood and to be despised.

However, you should not be discouraged by humiliation. This is the last hurdle your psychology has to overcome to ensure that no complex remains in your character and nothing limits your capacity for work and for service of God. The balm of optimism and confidence will act in such a way that the wound—cauterized by humility—may be healed perfectly and be turned into a trophy of victory. Despair and discouragement would do great damage to your ascetical struggle and to your life of apostolate. After reacting with humility of heart and avoiding, also with humility, the dangers I have just pointed out to you, we will raise ourselves up again, my friend, with great confidence. What a good starting point for our confidence is humiliation accepted with humility!

Let us feel with Saint Paul the strength and push of the virtue of hope; like the wind on the sea, it will fill the sails of the boat of our interior life: "When I am weak, then I am strong" (2 Cor 12: 10). Now that I am more aware of my weakness I will be able to use God's strength as my support. For this hope will reawaken our love, which has been asleep; and it will help us find suitable words to express that love to our Lord. To my mind, no words are more apt than those of Peter to Christ, words of contrite and confident love, at their first meeting after he had denied him three times: "Lord, you know everything, you know that I love you" (Jn 21: 15). You know, Lord, that I love you in spite of everything and above everything. And the weight that was oppressing us disappears, and of the humiliation nothing remains but humility, experience, and love.

Humility and hope lead our soul by the hand to joy and decision. How resourceful humility is! Our strength is increased; our decision has become stronger and more prudent. Joy will force us to repeat those encouraging words of Saint Paul: "I will all the more gladly boast of my weakness" (2 Cor 12: 9). And our decision spells itself out in those other words of the Teacher of the Gentiles: "I can do everything" (Phil 4: 13).

Conversation with the Virgin Mary, who is all humility, arises so spontaneously that I prefer not to write it down. I would rather your soul and mine spoke to her in private.

THE ROAD OF PRIDE

You have heard it said that the best business in the world would be to buy people for what they are really worth and sell them for what they think they are worth. . . . Sincerity is difficult. Pride overbears it, memory obscures it: facts disappear into thin air, or are embellished, and one is left with an attempt at justification aimed at giving an appearance of goodness to the evil one has done which one is not ready to correct; arguments and reasons are piled one on top of another—drowning the voice of conscience, which grows ever weaker and more confused.

JOSEMARÍA ESCRIVÁ DE BALAGUER, MARCH 24, 1931

THERE IS one road that definitely does not lead to salvation or happiness, and yet we take to it with great ease. It is the road of pride. Allow me, therefore, my friend, to say something about it, so that both of us can learn to recognize it immediately and always avoid it.

The road of pride has a rather sad beginning, for it starts with denying God in our souls and in our lives. In this connection, someone has very acutely observed that the atheist and the proud man have a lot in common. The atheist refuses to admit that the existence of God can be demonstrated from creation and created things: he does not see God our Lord in them. And the proud man refuses to recognize God in his soul and in his life: he does not see God our Lord in the gifts of nature and grace that enrich his personality and render his life effective.

Pride, really, is nothing other than a disordered evaluation of one's qualities and talents. It is nothing but the inflated and disordered idea that we have formed of ourselves. Freely and with a kind of interior circumspection we cultivate this exalted concept of ourselves; we admit to no shadow, however slight; we will refer our opinion of ourselves to no one else; and we will accept no reproach of criticism. We attribute to ourselves—forgetting completely about God our Lord—all that we are and all that we are worth. And by acting in this way we exclude God and other people from our life: *Only I matter,* the proud man obstinately claims; he is full of himself.

In souls who take the road of pride, there is no echo of those words of Saint Paul: "What have you you did not receive?" (1 Cor 4: 7). Nor will they surrender in the face of those other words that round off the Apostle's case: "If then you received it, why do you boast as if it were not a gift?" If there is any road that makes souls complicated, it is the road of pride. It is a labyrinth in which they completely lose their bearings. Pride destroys a soul's simplicity: simplicity—being and appearing to be without creases or folds (*sine plicis*)—simplicity, which is such a charming characteristic of humble people.

How many creases are formed, however, in the soul contaminated by pride! This capital sin induces a person—ever more imperiously—to keep turning in on himself: a thousand times folding in on himself and thinking about his own talents, his own virtues, his own successes, or about this or that occasion when he came out on top. This is the empty, mean world of vain self-satisfaction.

The road of pride runs implacably from a person's interior world into the external world. Everything these people have built inside themselves, they now want to construct in their environment as well. Even though the Lord said, "I will not give my glory to another," the proud soul replies to this divine commandment by appropriating, by taking over, that very glory.

This sorry road can never go anywhere near where the Lord is to be found. Nothing and nobody can make souls who have taken this road say, "By the grace of God I am what I am" (1 Cor 15: 10). They never look or think about anything higher than their own qualities and their own successes; they never look up at God our Lord, to thank him for his goodness. The road of pride begins by excluding God and folding in on oneself.

The proud person's horizon is terribly limited: it stops at himself. He can see no farther than himself, his qualities, his virtues, his talent. His is a Godless horizon. Even other people have no place on this cramped horizon: there is no room for them. Because of the high opinion he has formed of himself, the soul who follows this road never asks anyone for advice and never accepts any advice. He is self-sufficient. He is fixed in his own opinions and his self-will to the point of stubbornness, and he voluntarily ignores and even despises any opinion or conviction not his own. People who follow this road usually have a low opinion of others. They have become pharisees, and they regard other people as publicans. They reproduce continuously in their own lives the Gospel parable: "I thank you that am not like the rest of men" (Lk 18: 11). The "rest" exist only as something the paragon measures himself against—so that he can raise himself up and despise others.

People who follow this road will not admit that anyone is superior to them. That possibility does not exist, not even hypothetically. Others have no function but to exalt the proud man: they are way down below. The defects of other people are used to prove and underline the proud man's quality. The mistakes others make only emphasize his cleverness and competence; and the limited intelligence of others only make his intelligence shine forth. Here we find the root of the envy, jealousy, and anxiety that are features of the life of all those who follow the road of pride.

But this unfortunate road does not end there. Envy turns into enmity. How many enmities have their origin—strange origin!—in envy. There are people who are despised, hated, and attacked for the simple reason that they are better or more intelligent than their persecutors. They are accused of the great crime of being good or intelligent, or of having worked hard. And this crime is assailed and punished—on the road of pride— by coldness, enmity, silence, and calumny.

The proud person won't give an inch; he will resort to lies and hypocrisy to hold on to what he has. Everything is lawful, everything is good, on this cursed road, provided one is out in front and is the best in one's own opinion and in that of others.

If we are always to stay far away from this road, or to leave it should we find ourselves there, let us ask our Lady—the Teacher of humility—to help us understand that the beginning of all sin is pride.

CELIBACY AND CHASTITY

. . . our chastity is a joyful affirmation, a logical consequence of our surrender to God's service, of our love.

JOSEMARÍA ESCRIVÁ DE BALAGUER, MARCH 24, 1931

CHASTITY, my friend, perfect chastity, which I want to speak to you about today, is the other side of the coin of love. A simple example, taken from human love, will help us understand and strengthen our hold on the meaning this virtue should have for us. When one person really loves another and loves her to the extent of wanting her to be his companion for life, this love is and should be necessarily exclusive: this love fills his heart, his whole life, and logically excludes other loves incompatible with it.

In the world is the same heart with which we have to love God our Lord, and this same heart we give to the clean, noble loves of the earth is the heart you and I have given to Jesus. We have followed him, joyfully renouncing other affections, which, though they are human affections, do not cease to be fine ones. Those who followed an earthly love had their eyes open and their hearts full; and we, who have followed a heavenly love, also had our eyes open and our hearts full. And this love of God that finds expression in celibacy and perfect chastity is likewise exclusive and forbids any other love incompatible with it.

Nothing or no one is more lovable than Jesus Christ, Saint Paul has said; it is a conviction repeated by all who have renounced all the things of the earth, even quite lawful things, in order to follow Jesus more closely. With Saint Paul they evaluate human things by saying, "I judge everything as refuse, in order that I may gain Christ" (Phil 3: 8). My brother, let us regard celibacy and love for perfect chastity as exigencies (for you and me) of our love for Jesus Christ. Our soul, our heart, and our body are his; we have given them to him with our eyes open. And let's not forget that we do not need and cannot need anything: *Deus meus et omnia:* My God and my all!

I cannot tell you—because it would be not quite right—that chastity, purity, takes first place among the virtues, because you know perfectly well (I only want to remind you) that the first virtue, beginning with the foundations, is faith. That virtue is the basis of our whole spiritual edifice. You also know that the first virtue, looking at the structure from the top down, is charity, for only through charity—the queen of virtues—are we united directly to God.

And yet it would not be right if I did not add here that chastity, purity of life, provides the setting, the climate, suitable for the development of those two virtues and, along with them, all the other virtues. So it is not difficult to understand how important and necessary this virtue is in the spiritual life. Without this virtue, which creates the right climate, we would never be men and women of interior life; without this virtue, practiced conscientiously and professed joyfully and lovingly, we could not possess a truly supernatural life. The sensual man is the antithesis of the spiritual man; the carnal man cannot perceive the things of the spirit, the things of God; he is a prisoner of the earth and of the senses, and he will never be able to rise to enjoy the good things of heaven and the spiritual joys, the deep, serene joys, of the soul.

Chastity is also very necessary for apostolate. Celibacy and perfect chastity give the soul, the heart, and the external life of those who profess them that freedom which the apostolate needs so much if it is lavishly to serve the good of other souls. This virtue, which makes men spiritual and strong, free and agile, helps them to see around them souls and not bodies, souls who hope for the light of their word and their prayer, and the charity of their time and their affection. We should have a great love for celibacy and chastity because they are concrete and tangible proofs of our love of God and are at the same time sources that make us continuously grow in that same love—all of which makes us appreciate how much our interior life grows and how effective our apostolate becomes through these sacrifices full of love.

I wish to remind you now of a very simple truth, a truth we know, which we have often heard and taught. Chastity is possible, chastity is always possible, at all times, at all ages and in all circumstances, even when temptations and difficulties abound. Chastity is possible, not because our own limited strength can make it so, but because the goodness of God maintains us in it through his grace. All souls who pray and who strive to live "as angels of God" have experienced the certainty and the consoling truth of those words which Saint Paul heard: "My grace is sufficient for you" (2 Cor 12: 9).

And following this simple, smooth route, recalling truths that you and I know and love, I shall pause for a moment to examine a concept that cold hearts and minds unenlightened by faith bring us to consider. I cannot hide from you, my friend, that it causes me pain to pause even to think that perhaps among our brothers, among those of us who have given our Lord the gift of our youth and our life, there may be someone who thinks that perfect chastity is a form of mutilation, a sacrifice that renders a person incomplete.

Let me confide in you that I have known, with sadness, some of these souls, who carry on their shoulders the weight of a chastity they feel to be less beautiful and less fruitful than marriage. You know that this feeling is not shared by our Mother the Church; in going astray, they have for company the sadness of a barren life.

Perfect chastity is indeed a renunciation; we know this, and we have no wish not to know it: perfect chastity is a renunciation of the pleasures of the flesh, it is a renunciation of married love, and it is a renunciation of parenthood. But it is a renunciation full of light and love. It is a renunciation of love, because— I repeat—love is by nature exclusive, and he who loves in no way deprives himself when he deprives himself of everything which is not his love. And when this love is God, when this love is Christ, the exclusivity not only does not hurt, it enchants. The emptiness of this renunciation is filled in a wonderful, overflowing way by God himself: the love of God makes us happy and fills us—we lack nothing.

Chastity is love, an exclusive love of God, a love that does not weigh upon us, a love of God that makes us light and agile, and which at the same time fills us with a deep and serene happiness. And because chastity is love, we should repeat with our lives— which are always young and full of the enthusiasm of people who are in love—those words with which a spiritual lover concluded a series of beautiful pages written about this virtue: we have defended our right to love.

With our deep, clear conviction of the meaning and beauty of this virtue; with our firm and actual decision, which will make us repeat and affirm that we would do it over again a thousand times because we are convinced that it is the very best thing we could have done; with our eyes and our hearts set on Jesus Christ, to whom we have entrusted our lives, we can truly say that we have defended our right to love. I will go farther, using the happy expression of a poet monk: we are the aristocrats of love in the world.

And I need not tell you, because I have told you already, that chastity cannot be a tolerated virtue; chastity should be for us a virtue that we assert joyfully, love passionately, and guard vigorously and with refinement.

If we see purity in this way, as the fruit and source of love, we will consolidate it in our lives; we will love it and look after it in all its breadth and greatness. God our Lord asks us for purity of body, of heart, of soul, and of intention.

Purity, my brother, is a fragile virtue, or, better, we carry the treasure of this virtue "in fragile vessels" (2 Cor 4: 7); that is why it needs prudent, intelligent, and refined keeping.

But to keep this virtue and to defend it, we have invincible weapons—our humility, our prayer, and our watchfulness. Humility is the disposition we need for God to grant us this virtue: "God gives his grace to the humble" (1 Pet 5: 5). There is no doubt that the union existing between these two virtues, between humility and chastity, is very intimate. Even to the point that I once was pleased to read that a spiritual writer called humility "chastity of the spirit."

But neither should we forget that, in order to defend this virtue and to grow in it, it is absolutely necessary for us to listen to Jesus' advice: "Watch and pray" (Mt 26: 41). This watchfulness will lead us to flee decisively and immediately from the danger and opportunity of unfaithfulness. It will also show itself in the moment of our opening ourselves, sincerely and filially, to spiritual direction. It will teach us to mortify our senses and our imagination.

Prayer, friendship with Jesus in the blessed Eucharist, the sacrament of penance, and devotion to our immaculate Mother are the effective and necessary means of securing the virtue of chastity.

TRUE AND FALSE VIRTUES

*Our Lord usually leads beginners—sometimes for a period of years—
through these less choppy waters, in order to confirm them in their first
decision; he does not want to demand of them, early on, what they cannot
give, for they are* quasi modo geniti infantes, *like newborn babies.*

JOSEMARÍA ESCRIVÁ DE BALAGUER, MARCH 24, 1931

WHEN SOULS take their first step on the road of the spiritual life,
it's usually like that little fellow who has planted a grain of
wheat in the corner of the garden late one evening, or a peach
stone, and very early the next morning runs out to see what's
happened, expecting to find a fully grown shoot of wheat or to
be able to enjoy ripe peaches.

And then, when he sees that the earth is not fertile enough to
satisfy his hopes or his childish whims, he runs off, all tears,
looking for his mother to tell her how cruel the garden is to
have deprived him of the reward of his efforts. And his mother
smiles at him tenderly.

Well, just like that child, for whom a night's waiting seems
like years, there are very many people who expect their soul to
produce the fruit of solid, genuine virtue when they have hardly
planted the seed of good resolutions and have watered it merely
with a desire for holiness and faithfulness.

When some difficulty or obstacle arises, these souls learn very
quickly that their virtue is not as strong or as exuberant as they
liked to think it was; and then they become sad and discouraged.
And God our Lord, who loves these souls as a mother loves her
little child, smiles at the childishness of their interior life.

My friend, it is absolutely necessary—from the word "Go"
—for us to get used to seeking genuine, true virtues and to
learn to avoid false virtues. Yes, you have begun, and you have
begun well. It is true that the *"Nunc coepi:* I am beginning
now!" has found a generous echo in your life; but it is also
true—and you sometimes forget this—that genuine virtues
(which are good habits) require time and work, striving and effort. Good resolutions, ardent desires, are not enough; they

won't produce solid, genuine virtues. Nor will they, of themselves, change your personality and your character. For your virtues to become solid, for your character and personality to be transformed, you have to make a persevering effort right through all that period of work and struggle, which is your life.

Ardent desires and devout feelings, which usually, because of God's providential goodness, accompany one's first steps in the practice of the interior life, lead souls who are still very much newcomers to believe that they have already arrived, that their disordered defects and tendencies have disappeared, and that from now on everything is going to be easy. The virtuous life is not going to cause them to lose any feathers.

But God's providence, through their very experiences of life, will quickly open their eyes and will show them what the spiritual life and maturity of virtue really involve. Life itself will teach them that all those defects and tendencies are not dead at all; they are merely asleep, and it will need a really persevering effort and a lot of faith to give them a proper deathblow. When God our Lord takes those souls who want to follow him closely and leads them from sensible devotion to dryness and on from that to genuine spiritual devotion, that is when they come to understand God's plans and the stratagems he uses to help them acquire true virtues and a good, solid formation.

I still remember how happy I was to learn from a holy religious this simple, instructive proverb: "The young look like saints, but they are not; the old don't look like saints, but they in fact are." Young people's enthusiasm to follow Jesus closely is a budding flower, a promise; but the serene, deep, intensive work of souls in the service of God is ripe fruit, something really effective.

To want an effortless holiness, to look for virtue without being tested, without striving, without battles or defects—this is a youthful dream that cannot stand up to the experience of genuine spiritual life. There are, on the other hand, virtues that develop in the midst of difficulties; virtues that take root, through time and effort; virtues that, after much effort and many victories, acquire the promptness, ease, and constancy proper to genuine virtue. All these characteristics, along with a spiritual taste for the practice of virtuous acts, are a proof and a confirmation that a virtue is genuine.

And it is precisely to help you reach this goal that God our Lord puts you to the test in your prayer, with all that dryness; in your apostolate, with that apparent barrenness. He tests your humility, by means of humiliation; your faith and trust, through difficulties; your patience, through tribulation; your charity, through the defects and shortcomings of others and also through being crossed by good people. Genuine virtues have to grow and develop through your confident effort and your calm patience. Remember: "Through patience, through endurance, you shall possess your souls" (Lk 21: 19); patience is the price of holiness.

God our Lord does not want your virtues to be like hot-house plants: they would not be real virtues. Everything we have been meditating about together has shown us the way to genuine virtue and has also taught us that virtues, when they are genuine, have a solidity all of their own, which does not depend on external encouragement or shoring. Genuine virtues are at home in the world (without becoming absorbed in the world); they develop in the context of ordinary life and in the midst of difficulties, just as the rays of the sun dry out the ground without themselves being soiled. Genuine virtues knit together the life of the person who practices them. False virtues lead to that terrible separation between life of piety and everyday life. False virtues form separate, watertight compartments in one's daily round; they fail to irrigate a person's whole life. There are people who seem to be good in certain circumstances or at certain times of the day or week, because that's their custom, or it's easier that way.

False virtues are like gilded tin, which looks like gold at a distance, but the moment you take it in your hands you know it's a fake; and if you scratch ever so slightly, you will see the tin under the thinnest layers of gold. On the other hand, genuine virtues are gold, pure gold, without dross, even though sometimes this pure gold may be stained by specks of tin. But our Lord takes this pure gold in his hands, removes these specks, and allows the precious metal to shine in all its splendor.

May the Virgin Mary, the Queen of virtues, teach us to desire and to practice true virtues!

SERENITY

Ascetical struggle, putting into practice, right through the day, the theological virtues, which are virtues to be lived before being theorized about—faith, hope, charity. . . . That is the way to have serenity. Serenity: which is a layman's way of describing one of the results of fortitude, temperance, justice, prudence—of the cardinal virtues.

JOSEMARÍA ESCRIVÁ DE BALAGUER, MAY 31, 1954

WHEN I WAS small, like all children I used to build little forts out of mud and stones and bits of wood; and if anyone walked on them and knocked them down . . . I was really annoyed. What a catastrophe! I am amused now to think back on it; I can only smile at those childish catastrophes. Yet, if we look at them supernaturally, very many of the preoccupations of much older people and apparently very mature people are in the same category as children's games and childish catastrophes.

The virtue of serenity is a rare virtue; it teaches us to see things in their true light and evaluate them properly. Their real, objective value is shown us by balance and common sense; and our spirit of faith indicates the supernatural value they should attain. This serenity is missing when we deform reality, when we turn a molehill into a mountain, when things that should not cause us worry in fact do so—each and every time we fail to take account, in our judgments, of divine providence and the eternal truths. If we brought into our lives the Christian virtue of serenity, what would remain of all these worries, anxieties, and surprises? Nothing, or almost nothing.

Isn't it true that the mere passage of time means that we can, almost always, look serenely at the past; and, on the other hand, that only virtue can ensure we have a serene attitude toward the present and the future?

What happens is that time, as it goes by, leaves everything in its place. That affair or that event, which caused us so much worry, now that it's all over, it is barely a shadow, a *chiaroscuro* on the general canvas of our life. Well, it is about this serenity in relation to the present and the future that I want to talk to you. We need serenity of mind to avoid being slaves of our nerves or victims of our imagination; we need serenity of heart if we are to avoid being eaten up by anxiety or anguish; we need serenity in the way we act, to avoid darkness and empty-headed waste of energy.

A serene mind makes a person firm and steady, well able to direct others. A serene mind finds the right word at the right time to bring light and consolation, and it enables one to understand things properly and have a sense of perspective, to distinguish the woods from the trees.

I think I should say it again: the virtue of serenity is a rare virtue, for many people's lives are ruled by their nerves. Many are eaten up by their imagination, and there are some who turn everything into tragedy or melodrama.

The meticulous, persnickety person sees only details and is so insistent that he suffocates you; the theoretical type can see nothing but general questions, and he withdraws from real life: only the serene person is able to see the whole and the parts and integrate them properly. A rigid person is not serene, for his rigidity takes him beyond what is just and reasonable and prevents him from giving due weight to circumstance, time, and place. A rigid person's lack of serenity upsets and oppresses other people. However, a weak person is not serene, either, because he never goes far enough, and because of his weakness he harms himself and other people. A weak person doesn't get in other people's way, but he fails to control events; he is ineffectual; he is at the mercy of the current.

Objectivity and a capacity to be specific; analysis and synthesis; gentleness and energy; a brake and a spur; an overview and an awareness of detail: all these things and many more combine to produce, in a harmonious synthesis, the Christian virtue of serenity. But neither you nor I nor anyone else can be serene unless we first fight: everyone has passions; imagination can disturb every mind; nerves exist in everyone's body; everyone is overly sensitive in some area; ignorance, error, and exaggeration are to be found in everyone's mind; and fear and trembling can lurk in every heart.

Self-control, balanced judgment; careful and serene reflexion; control of our nerves and imagination: all this requires effort and firmness—and perseverance. That is the price of serenity. Serenity should be second nature to the Christian; for no Christian can be unaware of the fact that the gift of faith is a principle of serenity and harmony.

On all this panorama we have been considering, which has been cleared and prepared by the whole range of human virtues that make for balance, realism, and common sense: on this whole scene, the virtue of faith, the true sun of the soul, should rise as over a range rich with promise, giving us a view of life and its various options that is full of serenity. It should show us a broad horizon rich in details. Through this serene vision, the heart will be at ease, the soul will find calm, and the mind will understand, with God's light, the meaning of many things, and this understanding will increase the serene tranquility of your life. Even those things you do not understand will be unable to disturb your soul, for the same faith will teach you that the cause of what you do not understand is always the goodness of God and his affection for man.

Christian serenity: you have hidden under the dark veil of faith. Christian serenity: you come down on the soul, bringing supernatural outlook, as the dew comes down on flowers with the first light of morning. Christian serenity: you hide in the words of Jesus: "Let not your heart be troubled; neither let it be afraid"; "What does it profit a man to gain the whole world if he suffers the loss of his soul?" Christian serenity: you fuse with the soul in prayer as the rain soaks into the earth in springtime. Christian serenity: you put down deep roots in the soul who learns to embrace and overcome sorrow through the spirit of faith. Christian serenity: you settle down in the soul when it nourishes itself on the body and blood of Christ. Christian serenity: you fill the soul who opens himself sincerely and trustingly to his spiritual director. Christian serenity: you are the most delicate gift Jesus gives to souls who are simple and uncomplicated.

My friend, our Father God wants us to be serene in the midst of the tests and difficulties of life—"constant in prayer, patient in tribulation, rejoicing in hope" (Rom 12: 12).

My friend, Jesus wants us to be serene in the face of death and in the face of life: "Whether we live or whether we die, we are the Lord's" (Rom 14: 8).

My friend, the Lord wants us to be serene in our everyday work, especially when it becomes hard and burdensome.

My friend, God our Lord wants us to be serene when, because of our position, we have to give other people help and advice.

My friend, Jesus Christ wants us to be serene when we are at our desk and have to face the problems and decisions our work involves.

And he also wants us to be serene in our sincere effort to be better: "by endurance you will gain your lives" (Lk 21: 19). You lack this serenity when you get annoyed with yourself and when you lose your peace on seeing that your progress in the ways of the Lord is slow. Do not forget that the light of serenity is what makes you understand that "no one becomes a saint all of a sudden." And do not forget that you will never find our Lord in noise and in interior confusion, for the Lord comes in tranquility.

Therefore, if your prayer is serene in its reflection, in its affections, and in its resolutions, it will produce better and more enduring results. So you must fill your apostolate with serenity: it is a great gift of God, this ability to give a sense of security and serenity to souls as they make their way to God.

And the Queen of serenity—we say it joyfully—is our heavenly Mother.

CRITICISM

I shall never tire telling you that anyone who has a duty to judge must listen to both sides, to both bells. "Is it that our law condemns a person without first having heard him and learned what he does?"—Nicodemus, that upright, noble, and loyal man, reminded the priests and the Pharisees who sought to kill Jesus.

JOSEMARÍA ESCRIVÁ DE BALAGUER, SEPTEMBER 29, 1957

THE PEOPLE, things, and events we come into contact with provoke us to form opinions, to make judgments. Our noblest endowment, a gift from the Lord, takes up a certain position *vis-à-vis* ourselves and our surroundings. Your mind and your sensitivity—and mine also—measure and evaluate every person, thing, or occurrence they come into contact with. This ability to evaluate and form a judgment increases in proportion to a person's depth and the seriousness with which he confronts events and goes about the job of living. The richer a person is, the more deeply he reflects on things; and the more serious he is about his life, the greater his ability to judge must be. Silly, frivolous people, people who get caught up in details or who live in an unreal world, people who don't do anything or who do too much: all these people, to their great misfortune, are losing or have lost their capacity to evaluate and form sound opinions.

God our Lord wants you, my friend, to be a man of sound judgment; he wants you to be able to assess people, situations, circumstances, and events with supernatural outlook and with a practical approach to life. Your capacity to form judgments full of supernatural spirit should increase and improve steadily. For this ability to judge things in a Christian way, serenely and objectively, protects us against ourselves and against our enemies—especially the enemies of the soul—and enhances our actions and our effort to help our friends.

But this ability to judge—which is so necessary, for without it it would be difficult to act with Christian strength and maturity—has certain limits. If you keep it and use it within those limits, you will get closer to God; if you allow it to overstep those limits and don't use it in a Christian way, you will go away from God. How often you criticize in an unchristian way—thus setting yourself at a distance from God and from other people! You become everyone's enemy; everyone avoids you. You are well on the way to cut and destroy other people.

I am going to show you a whole range of examples of critical spirit, and then ask you: Into which of these categories might you and I fit? There is the criticism that comes from moral collapse (which turns you into an enemy of God); this person is critical of everything because he would like to drag everyone down to his own position of failure. Ironic criticism is biting, frivolous, and superficial, always ready to make a joke even of the most serious and sacred things. Envious criticism grows out of self-concern and indignation; it is foolish and proud. Idiotic criticism jeers at everything; proud, overbearing criticism is merciless and is usually made up of the very worst ingredients; criticism stemming from ambition is disloyal, because it aims at focusing attention on oneself to the detriment of others. Sectarian criticism is prejudiced, partial, and unjust; it is the criticism that comes from someone who uses lies consciously and coldbloodedly. Criticism by someone who takes offense is bitter and stinging. Criticism coming from an upright man is constructive; a friend's criticism is pleasant and very apposite; a Christian's criticism is something that actually sanctifies.

For your criticism always to be that of an upright man, a friend, a Christian; for it to be constructive, pleasant, apposite, and sanctifying, you have to strive always to avoid criticism of the person himself and his intentions. You must always respect him; you must not intrude on the sanctuary of his person and his interior world. What do you know about his intentions, about his motives, and about that whole series of subjective circumstances that only God our Lord can know, who reads hearts? Here Christ comes to meet you when he says: "Judge not and you shall not be judged" (Mt 7: 1).

This kind of criticism, which is deeply human, because we know our limitations, is also deeply Christian, because it respects the sphere that belongs to the Lord, and so it helps build and maintain friendship—even friendship with people who are very different from ourselves, for it shows it is full of respect and understanding for the other person. An upright man, and therefore with more reason a Christian, never judges or criticizes what he does not know. If you are going to express a judgment, you have to know all aspects of the matter you are judging. All your seriousness and rectitude and justice would fall apart if you did not first have all the necessary facts.

On reaching this point, I am sure that both you and I remember many impoverished judgments and criticisms, which we made in complete ignorance of the facts: the judgment of a superficial man who speaks without knowing anything; the criticism issued by someone who relies on hearsay, without bothering to check his information; the behavior of that empty-headed type who offers opinions even on things he knows nothing at all about. And we are aware also how easily we turn a mere impression into a judgment without going through the proper stages that accurate criticism requires. An ignorant person's criticism is always unjust and harmful.

Criticism, Christian criticism, always has to meet certain requirements of time, place, and manner; otherwise it easily becomes detraction or defamation. In this connection, it would be good for you, who consider yourself a mature person able to form sound opinions, to ask yourself whether you in fact have that minimum Christian prudence which puts you on your guard against the danger you can do in speaking and writing. For, speaking and writing without careful reflection can be dangerous for your soul, even if you are right, even if what you say is true.

I should go farther, my friend, and remind you that criticism is colored by the animus that lies behind it, by the attitudes it stems from. There is a good animus and a bad animus; we should remember this, for it offers us a sound standard for assessing the use we make of our capacity to evaluate and judge. People who are failures, people who are envious, ironic, proud, overbearing, fanatical, embittered, and ambitious have a bad animus; it shows itself immediately. On the other hand, the honest man, the friend, and the Christian have a good animus, which is also apparent in their judgments. This good animus is charity, a wishing other people well, and it ensures that any criticism they make has the qualities good criticism needs. For, if criticism is to be just, constructive, effective, and sanctifying, you need to love other people, you need to love your neighbors. If you in fact do love them, then any criticism you make is always an act of virtue and a positive help to the person you address: "A brother helped by his brother has the strength of a walled city" (Prov 18: 19).

Knowing how to defend yourself against unjust and evil criticism is usually a virtue and almost always a duty; knowing how to receive and accept good criticism is also a Christian virtue—and a sign of wisdom. To let yourself be told things, to receive criticism joyfully and thankfully is a sure sign of spiritual greatness. A person who learns to listen and to ask will go far in putting his God-given talents to good use. But he is unfortunate who cannot bear being criticized or who, in wounded self-love, looks for a thousand ways to get his own back on someone who has had the kindness and charity of giving him good, honest criticism. We should never forget, you and I, that everything we do badly should be done well and that everything we do well can be done better; and if we are to go in that direction, we need not only goodwill, for our part, but also helpful criticism from others.

However, we should never be too worried about criticism, about "what people will say." For excessive, cowardly concern of that type could easily clip your wings, cramp your style, and lead you to do nothing. The best thing to do about envious, gossipy, superficial criticism is to ignore it. I should like to tell you in this connection that he who does nothing will never be criticized: for some reason or other, people rarely criticize someone who does nothing. Whereas he who does things, he who does a lot, is always criticized—by everyone: he is criticized by those who do nothing, because his life and work seem to point an accusing finger at them; he is criticized by those who act differently from himself, because they see him as a kind of opponent; and he is also criticized by people who seem to be good but who show they are bad by criticizing him for doing the same or apparently the same as they do themselves.

At other times you will find you are unjustly attacked and abused by people who think that no one can do anything good unless he calls on their help. When that happens, smile elegantly and keep working away.

Do not forget to thank God for all these things; and be grateful especially for honest, good, friendly, Christian criticism: be grateful both to God and to that person who has criticized you.

TEMPTATIONS

*Your feet of clay will not crumble, for you know the stuff you are made of
and you will be prudent; you know very well that only God can say,
"Which of you can accuse me of sin?"*

JOSEMARÍA ESCRIVÁ DE BALAGUER, MARCH 24, 1931

HOW DIFFERENT is our road, Lord—the road your disciples have
to travel—compared with the one we imagined for ourselves in
our youthful inexperience and in the golden dreams of our restless imagination! We used to see before us a quiet road, made up
of constant interior calm and easy external triumphs . . . and
also—why not?—some marvelous, noisy battles, and wounds
garlanded with laurels and then . . . the applause of the crowd.
We used to think, Lord, in a naïve and not very supernatural way,
that the mere decision to follow you and walk generously with
you, renouncing many noble and lawful human consolations,
would have changed our nature and left us free—as angels!—of
the weight of tribulation and the on-rush of temptation.

But your judgments, O Lord! are not ours, nor are our ways
like your ways. Our experience is a wonderful fabric in which,
in an apparently capricious way, events that are vehicles of your
will interweave with the divine attributes of your goodness,
your wisdom, your omnipotence, your divine knowledge, and
your mercy. This experience has taught us to understand and
relish the fact that the life of the Christian is warfare—"Life on
earth is a war" (Job 7: 1)—and that all your disciples have to
experience the *pax in bello:* peace in the midst of war—that
serving you produces. We will thank our Lord because, gently
and vigorously, he has taught us the supernatural value and the
providential purpose of temptations and tribulations. For, by
means of them, God has given our soul the experience of the
mature man, the hardness and realism of the veteran toughened
in battle, and the spirit of prayer of the most contemplative of
monks.

Temptations: you will have temptations! Your life of service of God and of the Church will necessarily include temptations; for your vocation, your calling, your generous decision to follow Jesus do not immunize your soul from the effects of original sin, nor do they stamp out once and for all the fire of your concupiscence, which is where temptation catches you out: "every man is indeed tempted by his wrong desire" (Jas 1: 14).

But you will console yourself by remembering that the saints—men and women of God—have fought the same battles as you and I have to fight to show our love for the Lord. Listen to Saint Paul's cry: "Who will free me from this body of death?" (Rom 7: 24). Think of the temptations of Saint Jerome during his austere and penitent life in the desert; read the life of Saint Catherine of Siena, and you will see the trials and difficulties of that great soul; and don't forget the martyrdom of Saint Alphonsus di Liguori, at the age of eighty; or the strong temptations to despair in the life of Saint Francis de Sales when he was a student; or the sorely tested faith of that apostle the Abbé Chautard . . . or the temptations of all kinds that so very many have suffered.

Let us reflect on them, my friend, with supernatural spirit: by means of temptation, provided you do not go looking for it imprudently, God our Lord tests and purifies your soul, "like gold in the furnace." Temptations strengthen and impress a seal of genuineness on your virtues: for what genuineness can be attributed to a virtue if it has not been strengthened by victory over the temptations it meets? "Virtue is forged in weakness" (2 Cor 12: 9). In temptation your faith is awakened and strengthened; your hope grows and becomes more supernatural; and your love—the love of God, who makes you resist bravely and not give in—expresses itself in an effective and affective way.

Besides how much experience you gain in your struggle against temptations—experience that will serve you to help, direct, and console many souls who are tempted and troubled—the need to have recourse to God, which you feel so strongly in those moments, will ensure that your life of prayer is deeply rooted in your soul. How you will grow in humility and in self-knowledge when you see your tendencies and your inclinations! Your merits will increase . . . and—why not?—you will find consolation in the prospect of a wonderful hope of heaven: he who sows in tears will reap in joy.

All these considerations will increase your confidence and your supernatural outlook. However, I want to add something: the greatest danger tempted and troubled souls are up against is discouragement, the fact that they can think that the temptation is too much for them, that there is nothing to be done, that the Lord has abandoned them, that from now on they have already given in. My friend, be watchful and strong against this particular temptation, which usually comes after one has fought valiantly: it is the strongest temptation and the one most to be feared.

Listen to me. You can always win! "I can do everything" (Phil 4: 13). If you fight and use the means available to you, victory is yours. To those who do what they can, God does not refuse his grace. God made Saint Paul understand this in the moment of temptation: "My grace is sufficient for you!" (2 Cor 12: 9). Grace! Never forget the grace of God. Our Lord knows perfectly up to what point you can resist, and also he knows, like the potter, the degree of temptation necessary for his "vessels of election" (Acts 9: 15) to acquire the degree of solidity and beauty that he has planned for them.

Never lose confidence, never be demoralized, never become alarmed. I remind you that to feel is not to consent, that the spontaneous tendencies of your body do not depend on your will. All you have to do is resist generously: only the will can give consent and admit sin into the soul. As long as you hold out, whatever happens, the Lord is with you, in your soul, even though you do not feel his presence. He is with you—more than ever, now when you are fighting—and he is saying to you, "It is I; do not be afraid" (Mt 14: 27).

Open ever wider the eyes of your soul: the Lord allows temptation, and he uses it providentially to purify you, to make you holy, to detach you more from the things of the earth, to lead you where he is and by the route he wants you to take, so as to make you happy, in a life that may not be comfortable, so as to give you maturity, understanding, and effectiveness in your apostolic work with souls, and . . . above all, to make you humble, very humble.

Listen now, with the new outlook these considerations may have given you, to these words of holy Scripture: "My son, if you aspire to serve the Lord, prepare yourself for temptation"

(Sir 2: 1). And you—a tempted and troubled soul—marvel at the goodness of God, who makes you relish, with hope of heaven, these words of the Holy Spirit: "Blessed is the man who suffers temptation, for because he has borne it he will receive the crown of life" (Jas 1: 12). Temptations will weave your crown!

But do not forget, my friend, that you need weapons in this spiritual battle. And your weapons have to be these: continuous prayer; sincerity and frankness with your spiritual director; the holy Eucharist and the sacrament of penance; a generous spirit of Christian mortification, which will bring you to fly from the occasions of sin and to avoid idleness; humility of heart; and a tender and filial devotion to our Lady, comforter of the afflicted and refuge of sinners. Always turn confidently to our Lady, and say: "My Mother, I trust in you."

IMAGINATION

Our method of teaching consists in being positive, not negative, and it can be summed up in two things—acting with common sense and with supernatural sense, supernatural outlook.

JOSEMARÍA ESCRIVÁ DE BALAGUER, MARCH 24, 1931

A PRUDENT PERSON would never choose a madman as an adviser on the most delicate problems of his life. If anyone acted like that, we would regard him as imprudent and silly. This truth, which is self-evident in ordinary life and in business, is not so clear, at least in practice, as far as the interior life and sanctification go. The imagination is a madwoman—*la loca de la casa,* Saint Teresa called her, with her usual wit—and yet how often we choose her, more or less consciously, as our adviser in the most delicate problems of our soul.

This madwoman confuses us with her fussing and distracts us with her chatter; she injects us with her various fears and makes us apprehensive; she whispers her baseless suspicion in our ears, tyrannizes over us with her ambition, and infects us with her envy. This madwoman makes us walk away from reality, leading us into a dreamworld, full of elation or pessimism; subtly she feeds us with the poison of sensuality and self-love. She is—we know from experience—the great enemy of our interior life; she is the eternal ally of the world, the flesh, and the devil. It is she who disturbs your prayer life and makes you fear mortification; who introduces into your soul the temptation of the flesh and of pride; who gives you a false idea of God and deprives you of a supernatural outlook; who lulls you asleep with frivolities or drowns you in the lethargy of lukewarmness; who puts out the flame of charity or kindles the flame of distrust and discord.

She is as wild as a horse without a bridle, as giddy as a butterfly. If you fail to control and guide her, you will never be a supernatural and interior soul. If you do not control her, you will never enjoy the serene calm so necessary for loving God. If you don't put a brake on her, you will never have that realism which a life of holiness requires. Calm, realism, serenity, objectivity: these are virtues born where the tyranny of the imagination is buried; virtues that grow and bear fruit in the ascetical effort of dominating and controlling your imagination. I was saying that the imagination is tyrannical. So tyrannical, that it twists our mind, misrepresents situations, and distorts our view of other people.

The Gospel offers a very eloquent proof of this tyranny. We are on the lake of Genesaret, and it is a dark, stormy night; the apostles have to row hard, against a violent wind. Their little boat, battling the waves, contains twelve men striving to resist the impetuous wind. Jesus has gone away to be alone on the top of a nearby mountain, to pray. But at the fourth watch of the night, Jesus approaches the apostles, walking on the water (Mt 14: 25). And the twelve, when they see Jesus walking on the water, become worried and cry: "It is a ghost!" You see: the adorable figure of the Master, who comes out to be with them, and help them, and calm the storm, silencing the waves with his imperious word, takes on, in their imagination, the appearance of a ghost, which fills them with fear and disquiet.

How often this Gospel episode is repeated in our own life! How often our soul, victim of our imagination, is frightened and uneasy! Those imaginary crosses that torment us and exhaust us: they are tricks our imagination plays on us. I don't think I exaggerate if I say that ninety percent of our sufferings, of those sufferings which, so little do we know the cross of Christ, we call crosses, are imaginary; or at least they are exaggerated or twisted by the cruel tyranny of our imagination. That is the reason why they weigh so heavy on us and drain us of energy, these human and invented crosses.

If what made us suffer so much, if what drained us, were truly the cross the Lord sends us, Jesus' cross, once we recognized it as such and, with faith and love, accepted it, it ought no longer to be a weight, it ought no longer to oppress us. For Jesus' cross, the holy cross, is not a source of sadness or depression, but of peace and joy. However, if it is a human or imaginary cross we are carrying on our shoulders, or one that is the result of our interior rebellion against the true cross, then indeed we become sad and worried. But this weight and this preoccupation can disappear from your life and cease to drain you: all you have to do is open the eyes of faith and decide to clip the wings of your imagination.

Allow me to tell you that these human crosses, which are so heavy that they flatten you, have no real existence in your supernatural life: they exist only in your imagination. You are carrying on your shoulders a weight as atrocious as it is ridiculous—a weight you imagine to be a mountain but in fact is a grain of sand. They are ghosts created by your mind, bogeymen whom your imagination decks out in vivid colors, giving them huge, terrifying hands and swift, agile legs. These are what are chasing you and filling your soul with sorrow and agitation. A little assertion of your life of faith would be enough to make them disappear. Don't you see how easily they can be banished away?

Sometimes we allow other things to scare us, things that come from far away—fears about future dangers. We are afraid of things or of dangers that at present do not exist, and we don't know if they will ever happen; but in our imagination we see them as present, and this makes them appear even more terrible. A simple, supernatural reasoning process will get rid of them: because these dangers that you imagine possible are not actual dangers and because this fear you have has not been verified, then clearly you do not have the grace of God necessary to overcome them, to accept them. If your fears were verified, if things did turn out as you expect, then you would have divine grace; with that grace and your response to it you would win out and have peace.

It's quite natural that at present you do not have God's grace to overcome those obstacles and to accept crosses that exist only in your imagination. What you have to do is base your spiritual life on a serene, objective realism.

Even in the field of charity, you can often be the victim of your imagination! So much suspicion without any basis—a suspicion whose only roots are in your mind! How many things you imagine your neighbor to have thought or said or done, which he has never thought or said or done! This sort of thing disturbs and undermines your relationships with other people and your family life. Those little differences, which necessarily exist in all human relationships, even in those of the saints (for we are not angels), are blown up and twisted by our imagination and put us into moods that make us suffer greatly. Nothing, little things, and games our imagination plays on us: yet they open abysses that cause division among people, destroy affections and friendships, and undermine unity.

Imagination, moreover, is the great ally of sensuality and self-love. How many novels you devise for yourself—fantastic dreams in which you are the hero, the person who comes out on top; dreams that indulge your ambition, your desire to be on top and be admired, and your vanity.

There you are—so many obstacles to your holiness.

Your life of piety; your prayer; your presence of God; abandonment into the hands of our Lord; strong supernatural joy: all these walls of your interior life are threatened by the madwoman of the house.

Be supernatural, be objective. The voice of Jesus puts an end to the fears of the apostles on the lake of Genesaret: "*Ego sum, nolite timere:* Take heart, it is I; do not be afraid!" (Mt 14: 27).

EXAMINATION OF CONSCIENCE

. . . all our glory consists in the evidence, produced by our conscience, that we have acted in this world, with simplicity of heart and with sincerity before God.

JOSEMARÍA ESCRIVÁ DE BALAGUER, JUNE 16, 1960

IN THE SILENCE of examination of conscience I like to reflect on, and apply, these words of the sequence in the Mass for the Dead: "The book will be read out in which everything is written." When the moment comes for us to meet Jesus, the pages of the book of our life will be turned quickly before our eyes—the book containing everything we did during our lifetime.

So, to make sure that there are no surprises at the last moment, I often like to take this book in my own hands—this book that I'm in the process of writing, whether I like it or not, as long as I live. I like to take it up and open it and let my soul read it. And that's very easy and very useful to do at the time of prayer or of examining one's conscience. I like to think that every day of my life is a page of this book; and when I begin a day, what I have in front of me is a blank sheet of paper. And sometimes I run quickly through the pages already written and allow the blank pages to pass through my fingers—the pages not yet written because the time hasn't yet come. And, in a funny way, some pages always stay on my fingers: they are the days I don't know whether I'll get to write, because I don't know when the Lord will show me this book for the last time.

And these blank pages, on which we begin to scribble each day, I like to head up with just one word: *Serviam*. I will serve. It is both a desire and a hope. It is a desire because I sincerely do want each page to have that meaning. In other words, I want to serve God by writing properly and by writing what he wants me to write. It is a hope because with God's grace I trust that I will be able to do everything I want to do.

After beginning in that way—with that desire and that hope—I try to write words and phrases and make paragraphs and fill the page with neat, clear writing. That means work, prayer, apostolate—all my day's activity.

I try to give a lot of attention to punctuation—which is the practice of keeping the presence of God. These pauses—commas, or semicolons, or colons—represent the silence of my soul and the aspirations I try to use to give meaning and supernatural outlook to everything I write.

I particularly like the full stops, because after every full stop I begin, in a way, to write again. They are a kind of indication that I am correcting my intention, saying to our Lord that I'm going to start writing again: I'm going to start again with the right intention of serving him and dedicating my life to him, moment by moment, minute by minute.

I am also careful about putting in the accents, crossing my *t*'s and dotting my *i*'s—the little mortifications that give my life and my work a truly Christian meaning. When I omit an accent, it means that I did not accept in a Christian way the mortification our Lord was sending me, which he had lovingly prepared for me and wanted me to find and receive with pleasure.

I try to see that there is nothing crossed out, no mistakes or blots, no big gaps; but . . . there are so many! These are my infidelities, imperfections, sins . . . and omissions.

It hurts me to see that there is hardly a single page that has not some sign of my awkwardness and clumsiness. But I quickly console myself and calm down by remembering that I am only a little child who hasn't yet learned to write and has to use a ruled sheet under the page to help him write straight, and who needs a teacher to guide his hand so he doesn't simply scribble: what a good Teacher is God our Lord, what infinite patience he takes with me.

At other times I amuse myself by going back to the early pages in the book to see the scribbles—when all I could do was make a few strokes; and then the following pages, which have only letters, big, awkward letters, made by an unsure hand; and later on, I find words and short phrases and, on the more recent pages, continuous lines of good handwriting.

I do want, Lord, to learn how to write this book; I want to learn to let my hand be guided by your hand, so I can do your will at every moment. And I would like to fill every one of these pages with expressions full of sincere affection and love, or at least—when I don't manage to write what I ought—with sincere, serene words of contrition.

Playing with this book either saddens me or consoles me. Do you, my friend, want to join me in learning how to entertain yourself every day, sincerely, with depth and perseverance, by playing this game, which our Lord enjoys so much? The name of the game is examination of conscience. You will gain a great deal of knowledge of yourself and of your character and your life. You will teach yourself to love God and to affix your desire to make good use of your days by making clear, effective resolutions. And you will feel, as I now feel, a desire to write a canticle of love for God, "to sing the Lord a new song" (Ps 32: 3), a song that really will be a new song each day, because you will write it with a vivid awareness of your vocation, of your life as a son of God, which is each day renewed: "Behold, I make all things new" (Rev 21: 5).

Friend, take up the book of your life and turn its pages every day, so that you won't be surprised when it is read on the day of your particular judgment, and won't be ashamed when it is published on the day of the universal judgment.

IN OUR FATHER'S PRESENCE

*We are like children before God, and if we look on our ordinary life
(where everything is apparently the same) in the light of that fact, we
see the hours of our day take on new life: we will notice that they are
full of wonderful things, beautiful things, and all different.*

JOSEMARÍA ESCRIVÁ DE BALAGUER, MARCH 24, 1930

YOU WILL fill me with the joy of your presence" (Ps 15: 11). The
continuous practice of the presence of God is a sound, effective
way to achieve perfection. Living always with you, Lord, seeking
your presence, knowing that you are following everything we
do, and turning to you in all the little events that go to make up
our daily round: for a Christian, this recognition that one can
and ought always live in the presence of God is a constant
source of joy.

Lord, please make sure that our days are always filled with the
joy of your presence; no matter what difficulties crop up, no
matter what bad times we have to go through, give us the consolation of knowing that you are present with us. *"Horas non
numero nisi serenas"* (I mark only the peaceful hours): this in-
scription, which I saw on a sundial, describes the serene joy
given to those who walk in the presence of God—and they in
turn spread it to others. Awareness of the supernatural meaning
of life—this sun that rises over the horizon of the Christian
soul—will dispel, with all the force of faith, all the little worries
and anxieties of every day, leaving the soul with the serenity of
someone who can look at everything with the eyes of God.

My friend, when we practice this presence of God, which
even now, as we talk, the Lord is asking of us, we will learn to
direct all our actions to him and be less and less selfish in our
resolutions. *Deo omnis gloria:* all the glory of God—that will be
the standard to aim at in everything we do. Only then will we
learn to disappear by seeking the high ideal the Church pro-
poses to all Christians: ". . . that every prayer and work of ours
may always be begun by you and brought to a conclusion by

you." For only then will we be Christ's—when our whole life is his; only then will all our actions tend toward Jesus Christ as their beginning and their end.

Purity of intention is nothing other than presence of God: God our Lord is present in all our intentions. How free our heart will be of every earthly obstacle, how clear our vision and how supernatural our way of doing things when Jesus Christ really reigns in our intimate world and presides over all our plans and purposes. Then—I would remind you—your soul will have discovered the simple, clear formula for being holy in the middle of everyday life, for seeking Christian perfection in all spheres of human activity. You will be able to sanctify yourself at every moment; and you will lead everything to God our Lord.

Think about this: selfishness and sensuality, self-love and resentment will not be able to settle in your soul or be the motive of your actions; you will fight off every kind of enslavement and keep at bay the enemy of your holiness, who is always trying surreptitiously to sow cockle among the wheat. But there is no cockle in souls who live in the presence of God: everything about them is good wheat. And with Christ's help—he is the goal of, the whole reason for, our lives—you will shake off that sleepiness which makes it easier for the enemy to catch you; and you will be ever vigilant, ever attentive to the presence of the Lord.

Purity of intention: Christ present in our intentions . . . Once we set out on this road we will also learn the virtue of humility, for everything we do and even the way we do it will protest our humility: "Not to us, O Lord, not to us, but to thy name give glory" (Ps 113: 1).

This presence of God, sought serenely and held on to with determination, ought to be a source of deep, intimate joy— every day of your life.

"May the Lord be with you on your journey" (Tob 5: 21): these words of Tobias when he blessed his son really augur very well for your family life, your social life, your study, your everyday work, and even your leisure time and your rest.

And by going along in the presence of God, what a sense of security you have! By feeling that God your Father is looking after you, you become really determined to make an effort; and you feel sure of winning. When temptation presses you hard, this serene awareness of God's presence will turn into internal prayer, heartfelt petition; it will become a shout full of faith and hope—like the disciples at Emmaus: "Stay with us, Lord, for it is nearly evening and the day is almost over" (Lk 24: 29).

If you live in the presence of God, you will learn to be skilled in that rare wisdom which is self-control; you will learn to control and conquer yourself, and you will experience the joy of making life pleasant for the people around you. By following this route, my friend, you will arrive at great intimacy with our Lord; you will learn to call Jesus by his name and will come to love recollection. Frivolity, superficiality, and lukewarmness will disappear from your life.

You will be a friend of God; and in your recollection, in your intimacy, you will love to consider those words of Scripture: "God went to speak to Moses face to face, as a man speaks to his friend" (Ex 33: 11).

So ask the blessed Virgin, Mother of God and our Mother, to help you make a resolution—the firm, generous resolution to walk from now on in the presence of God, all the time.

THE BREAD OF LIFE

Never get used to celebrating or attending the Holy Sacrifice: approach it, rather, with as much devotion as you would if it were the only Mass in your life: realizing that there Christ himself is always present—God and Man, Head and Body, and therefore, together with our Lord, his entire Church.

JOSEMARÍA ESCRIVÁ DE BALAGUER, MARCH 28, 1955

YOU KNOW very well that Eucharist means "thanksgiving." So that is precisely the first, spontaneous impulse of the soul who stops to reflect, to meditate, on this mystery of faith, which is the Sacrament of the Altar. The words that spring out of our heart, in response to the presence of Jesus in the Eucharist, are words of gratitude: Thank you, Lord, for having chosen to stay here in the tabernacle. Thank you, Lord, for having thought about me and about all men—even those who would hand you over to the enemy—when you were being persecuted and abandoned, on the night of your passion. Thank you, Lord, because you want to be a doctor for my ailments, strength for my weakness, and bread for my hungry soul—the bread that gives life.

You and I know by experience how much good a good friendship can do someone: it helps him behave better, it brings him closer to God, it keeps him away from evil. And if a good friendship links us not merely to a good man but to a saint, the good effects of that kind of life are multiplied: contact and conversation with a holy person will leave us with something of his holiness: *cum sanctis, sanctus eris!* (if you mix with saints, you will be a saint yourself).

Well, then, think what can happen if you become a close friend of Jesus Christ in the Eucharist; think of the deep impression that can make on your soul. You will have Jesus as a friend, Jesus will be your friend. He—perfect God and perfect man—who was born and worked and wept; who has stayed in the Eucharist; who suffered and died for us! . . . And what a friendship, what intimacy! He nourishes us with his body and gives us his blood to take away our thirst: "My flesh is real food, my blood is real drink" (Jn 6: 56). Jesus offers himself to us in the mystery of the Eucharist, completely, totally—body and blood and soul and divinity. And the soul, at that moment of gift and abandonment, feels it can repeat the words of the Gospel parable: "Everything I have is yours" (Lk 15: 31).

The way of Communion—and frequent Communion—is in fact the easiest and shortest way to achieve transformation in Christ, to get to the point where Christ lives in me, as Saint Paul said (Gal 2: 20). Your soul needs Jesus, because without him you can—we can—do nothing: "Without me you can do nothing" (Jn 15: 5). He desires to come to your soul every day: he told you so, he told me so, in the parable of the great banquet—"he invited a large number of people" (Lk 14: 16)—and he said it again when he solemnly instituted the Eucharist: "I have longed to eat this passover with you" (Lk 22: 15).

Your soul and mine need the bread of the Eucharist, because they need nourishment, just as our bodies do, to persevere faithfully and with the right attitude in our everyday work—in our effort to become holy and to progress, every day, in knowledge of God and in the generous practice of the virtues.

Let me tell you, in confidence, that your soul cannot be nourished and cannot be satisfied by anything other than God. That's just how wonderful and noble the soul in grace is. If we could only grasp that, we would have eyes for nothing else in the whole world. Our Christian faith, which enlightens our mind and brings peace to our heart, teaches that the soul has been created in the image and likeness of God; that it has been redeemed by the blood of Jesus Christ; and that we ought to take for our nourishment his redeeming body and blood.

Don't be led astray by wrong ideas and false humility: the state of grace, a right intention . . . and then, after having listened to the prudent advice of a priest, go to the most holy Eucharist, even every day.

In this connection I like to repeat those words of Martha to Mary, when Jesus—after the death of Lazarus—came to that friendly house at Bethany: "The Master has come, and he is calling you" (Jn 11: 28). Answer his call; go to him: approach this mystery of faith with great faith, with the faith of the Canaanite mother and the woman with the hemorrhage or, at least, with the humble desire of the apostles: "Increase our faith!" (Lk 17: 5).

Approach the Eucharist with the firm hope of the leper and use his humble and confident words. Say to Jesus: "Lord, if you wish, you can make me clean" (Mt 8: 2). And if you then get sad because you remember your wretchedness, you can say to Jesus what the centurion said: "Lord, I am not worthy"—but carry on immediately like that simple man, and savor his confident hope: "but only say the word and my soul will be healed."

Go to the Eucharist with the love that Mary Magdalen had, in the house of Simon the leper. Like her, forget about everything around you: be there alone with Jesus, be totally attentive to him, and offer him the fire of your soul and the fervor of your will. And don't have any human respect or any false humility. He is with you, and he loves you. Make good use of the time you spend in thanksgiving; let your thanksgiving be like the hymn the apostles sang in the upper room after the institution of the Eucharist, as they were going out into the open air. And leave the church with your heart overflowing with joy and your soul full of optimism. And during the day, review often your response to Christ's "longing to eat this passover with you"; tell him how much you desire to receive him. Spiritual communion is solid, sanctifying food for eucharistic souls.

Our Lady is the Mother of fair love and faith and holy hope: ask her to help you grow in these virtues so that you are ever better prepared to receive the most holy sacrament of the Eucharist.

I WILL BE WITH YOU ALWAYS

Prayer, which frequently takes the form of a glance—looking at him and feeling that He is looking at you; at other times, it means considering the greatness of God and our littleness; at others, telling him in detail what He already knows very well, what can and may weary us, which is his glory, not our self-interest, because He is more concerned about us than we are ourselves.

JOSEMARÍA ESCRIVÁ DE BALAGUER, SEPTEMBER 29, 1957

ORATE, FRATRES! Pray, brethren! My friend, listen to and meditate on these words the priest says at Mass when he turns to the people, opening his arms in a gesture of charity, almost as if he were begging. . . . Using these same words, in the same tone of supplication, and with the strength of the deep conviction the Lord has put into my priestly soul, I want to say to you again during these moments of recollection: Pray, my friend . . . ; you need to pray; my brother, pray! Protect and encourage your spirit of prayer.

One of the great treasures the Church, our Mother, possesses is the prayer of her sons and daughters. She counts on your prayer; she needs it if she is to knit herself together again and grow. She stands in vital need of the silence and activity of your prayer. Let us, therefore, you and I, try to be imbued with this sense of responsibility; let us introduce into our life, into our daily activity, a little time allocated to mental prayer—if we don't do so already. And if in our day's plans we have already allocated a certain amount of time aimed at achieving intimacy with God, let us persevere in our resolution and improve in our life of prayer.

Do you remember that passage of sacred Scripture that tells about the great battle of the chosen people against the Amalekite. While the Hebrew army was fighting on the plain, Moses, the leader of Israel, prayed to God with his arms up-raised: as long as Moses' arms remained raised—that is to say, as long as his prayer to God was intense and persevering—victory shone on the men of Israel; but if Moses' arms grew tired and he lowered them, victory eluded the people of God. Then—you remember?—the two people who were with Moses made him sit down on some rocks and kept his arms held high until victory was complete and triumph assured.

You and I have to convince ourselves more and more (and that is what we are doing just now) that our prayer is *needed* for the Church to win her battles and for us also to win out in the daily battles of our interior life. This conviction will strengthen those upraised arms of ours, our life of prayer. Frequent meditation on the need for prayer will lead us, by the hand as it were, to seek serious, regular spiritual direction—to look for someone, a priest, who, through his words and his advice, can keep those arms of ours up, at times of difficulty or dryness. It will also encourage us to act in such a way that many other arms will be raised in persevering prayer; it will help us through an effective apostolate to hold up the arms of many other souls of prayer.

Let us listen again to the voice of the Church: *Orate fratres!* Pray, brethren! Pray! . . . We now feel the need for this resolution to pray and improve our prayer life to spread right through our soul.

But, my friend, our prayer has to be always very specific. Prayer which is specific, concrete, is the only kind of prayer that has a real influence on our life. It confronts problems boldly and looks, vigorously, for Jesus' light. It actively avoids the unconscious tendency we have to keep open the wounds of our self-love. It accepts the will of God and tries lovingly to fulfill it. It penetrates silently, fruitfully, all the nooks and crannies of our soul and all the moments of our day's activity. It does not turn into a cold sort of study or an empty and silly sentimentalism. It extinguishes the protests of our self-love and drives out envy, jealousy, and resentment.

My friend, we have to be specific, practical, in our prayer, in this raising of the mind and heart to God to adore him, thank him, and ask him for light and strength. I have known disorientated and miserable souls whose prayer had no roots at all in their ordinary life. At the beginning of their day they put Jesus into a little corner of their soul, but they would not let him interfere in any way in the rest of the day; it was something like those Sunday Masses at twelve o'clock that have little or no influence on the lives of so many Christians.

Through this concrete and fervent prayer of every day, your tendency to holiness will be rewarded and strengthened: "In my meditation a flame will burst out" (Ps 38: 4). You will come to know Jesus, and his doctrine will become very familiar to you, and you will also get to know yourself. By means of prayer, you will defend yourself against your enemies and win all your battles; you will be armed and will have the protection of Christ's breastplate, as the Apostle invites you: "Put on our Lord Jesus Christ" (Rom 13: 14). In your daily prayer you will discover the reason for your apostolate; *contemplata aliis tradere:* to pass on to others what you have meditated. Everything you say and all the advice you give in your apostolate of friendship and confidence will carry the seal of things experienced and proven, which is the seal of effectiveness and consistency.

Your life of prayer should be defended like a treasure; the Church needs it, because it is the sure basis of our personal holiness, and Christ was addressing everyone when he said, "We ought always to pray" (cf. Lk 18: 1).

The real enemies of your prayer are: your imagination—"the madwoman of the house" who upsets and distracts you with her twisting and pirouetting; your senses when they are awake and little mortified; your lack of advance preparation—if you want to, you can call it something else: dissipation—which is why you feel so far from God our Lord when you start your prayer; your heart, which you do not mortify that much . . . , which you do not purify that much, which is so little detached from the things of the earth, things that cake with mud the wings of your soul and prevent you from raising yourself up toward greater intimacy with God; that lack of effort and genuine interest, on your part, during those moments when you are face to face with God.

Before we finish, say again to Jesus, through the mediation of the Virgin Mary—who is mystical rose and singular vessel of devotion—those humble words, full of confidence, which the apostles spoke: "Lord, teach us how to pray!"

DEATH AND LIFE

A great Love awaits us in heaven; a love which does not betray, does not deceive; the fullness of love, of beauty, of greatness, of all knowledge . . . and without tiring us: it will fill us, and yet always leave room for more.

JOSEMARÍA ESCRIVÁ DE BALAGUER, MARCH 24, 1931

REMEMBER, man, that you are dust and to dust you shall return." And the priest, dressed in the violet vestments of penance, puts ashes on the bowed heads of the faithful.

The Church, the spouse of Christ, wants men to be mindful of death, so that they live in Christian readiness for that step. But the children of this world want to have nothing to do with death. They prefer to have death as an implacable enemy, hidden, alien; they prefer it to come unexpectedly, as a painful surprise. That is why they bury the corpses of their loved ones as quickly as possible and strive to wipe out everything that reminds them of death. And yet one of the great things about man is precisely that he knows he has to die. And the Christian also knows that death is the price of sin: "death came into the world through sin" (see Rom 5: 12).

A Christian should think about death; he should serenely meditate on this truth until he is quite familiar with it; he should learn to treat death as a sister full of light and experience, who can give him sound, disinterested advice. Seen in this way, death, Christian death, our good sister death—that's what Francis, the *Poverello* of Assisi, called her—will show us her serene face, which will not shock or scare us but will fill us with the sweetest of Christian virtues—the virtue of hope. "Life is changed, not taken away."

A feeling of joy fills the Christian when he reflects on this truth. Your disciples, Lord, those who love you and who live—or at least sincerely want to live—for you, know very well that death is the beginning of Life; it is the beginning of that meeting with you, the reward of their efforts and the crown won by their struggle. To your disciples, Lord, those words are very familiar that you spoke to the apostles when you were talking to them about their life and the short while they would spend here below: "Your sorrow will be turned into joy" (Jn 16: 20). And that is precisely what happens: the sorrow of the body and of the world is turned into the joy of the soul and of heaven when you live in a Christian way and think about death in a Christian way.

Don't dress death, in your sickly and not-very-supernatural imagination, with black drapes and decaying flowers: look at death joyfully, as the wonderful conclusion of the Christian adventure. It is the moment of meeting and embracing—forever—between the son and the Father, the brave soldier and his Captain, the lover and his Love, the redeemed and his Redeemer, the creature and his Creator, the good and faithful servant and the just and generous Master, the victorious athlete and his laurels: *Deus tuorum militum sors et corona, praemium*; God, you are your soldiers' prize, destiny, and crown of laurels.

For you and me, my friend, "to live is Jesus Christ"—Saint Paul tells us—"and death is gain" (Phil 1: 21). Together with this thought and this feeling of joy, remembering death also gives us a wonderful sense of detachment, for it teaches us how to renounce the things of the earth. When we think, in the light of death, about our life and the things around us, we discover the great wisdom contained in knowing how to live as someone "who has nothing yet possesses everything" (2 Cor 6: 10). What are wealth, honor, pleasures?—things that slip through our fingers like water, things we cannot bring with us farther than the portal of death.

Detachment. Let us live in such a way that those words of the angel of the Apocalypse, "time has come to an end" (10: 6), find us with our heart and our hands empty of the goods of the earth and full of God and of his goods. Let us learn to die, a little each day, through separating ourselves from everything that is not eternal. Do you know why men, when they reach their last hour, suffer and are in anguish? Because having lived quite forgetful of the words "I face death each day" (1 Cor 15: 31), they must do in half an hour what they ought to have done over their entire lifetime. How hard, how bitter, is this forced detachment, which no one can escape. "O death, how bitter is the reminder of you to one who lives at peace among his possessions" (Sir 41: 1). Whereas the Christian, the detached soul, dies savoring the truth of those words of the psalm: "How I rejoiced when they said to me: Let us go to the house of the Lord" (Ps 121: 1).

Death, my friend, also teaches us to love and live the truth, for death is the moment of truth. Imagine what realism and what love for the truth you will have in your interior life if the thought of death becomes familiar to your soul. The deceptions of self-love, the duplicity of hypocrisy, the hidden feelings of revenge, the excuses of sensuality, the injustices and lies of life, and the enticements of frivolity cannot resist the penetrating light of death. At that moment—and forever after—you will be exactly what you are at that moment in the presence of God; in your heart there will be no dark corner where you can hide things. If you desire that lies, deceit, duplicity, and injustice—which is also a kind of lie—should cease to dominate your interior life and the lives of others, think about death.

I will suggest to you a rule of conduct: what would you think of that person, how would you judge that other person, how would you solve that serious problem if you were the next to die and, immediately after, had to render an account to God for that thought, that judgment, that decision? Well, then: always act as you would act at that moment. Always ask yourself: *Quid hoc ad aeternitatem?* What is this worth, in the light of eternity?

Our life is always short, like that of "a wild flower" (Ps 102: 15), the Scriptures say, and like a shadow it passes fleetingly (cf. Wis 2: 5). What use are you and I making of this short life, this little time we have to live here below? If the end came for us now, would we be satisfied with the use we had made of our time and of the gifts we received from God?

Teach us, Lord, to count our days, so that we attain the wisdom of the heart, that wisdom by which we are convinced that only good works and the service of God have value for eternal life. We do not know "the day nor the hour"; so we have to live in readiness. We have to be ready to say to the Lord that we accept death, that we accept it when he wills it, in the way he wills it, and where he wills it, convinced that he will take us when we are ready, when our soul has reached that degree of holiness to which it was called. Let us live intensely, with a holy desire to make good use of time and of all the opportunities we get to sanctify ourselves; let us try to give every minute of our life an echo of eternity.

And let us finish by thinking about our Lady, about the "dormition" of our Lady. Let us ask her, the patron of a happy death, to grant us the grace to work and live thinking about Death, so that we can later die thinking about Life.

FRATERNAL CORRECTION

When you see your brother do something wrong, when you see him do something which could endanger his soul or reduce his effectiveness, speak to him clearly. He will be grateful to you.

JOSEMARÍA ESCRIVÁ DE BALAGUER, SEPTEMBER 29, 1957

THERE IS A passage in Saint Matthew's Gospel (18: 15) referring to our obligation to make fraternal correction. It cannot be read without feeling a certain surprise and unease. For it tells us how Christ lovingly imposed on us a duty we rarely do these days, despite the fact that we are so keen on frankness and sincerity; indeed, the times we live in try to claim frankness and sincerity as their typical qualities. Although the duty to make fraternal correction is not rooted in the virtue of sincerity, that virtue, like honesty, does is some way help us to practice this precept of the Gospel. The precept itself is based directly on charity.

For it is precisely in the light of charity that we come to understand Christ's words and what this Gospel precept entails. We have to love our neighbor and wish him well; we have to desire his welfare, especially his eternal welfare; so we cannot remain indifferent, we cannot turn our back on anyone who is in danger, who has not taken the right road or who is not as good as he ought to be or could be. That is also why we have to make sure we do not simply close our eyes when we see someone, in our circle of friends and relations, who is on the point of breaking, or who already has broken, the order and harmony of charity. In this situation, as in many others, Christ's words oblige us not to close our eyes. For he tells us, "Go and correct him, alone. If he listens to you, you have won back your brother." His commandment has all the depth of simple things, the instant freshness of a practical approach.

The pages of Scripture teach us how, long ago, God made use of prophets, souls full of fortitude and charity, to warn men, even kings, when they had strayed. How faithfully and charitably those prophets fulfilled their duty to give fraternal correction! Well, then, in our own times, is there a less pressing need for this spiritual work of mercy, of giving advice to our brother who had made a mistake, or telling him something he should know? Yet it almost seems as if those words of our Lord, "Go and correct him," have not even touched the conscience of people; we scarcely notice the evil around us, an evil that could be avoided. For many of us, our "neighbor" is only the "people next door," and "others" are no longer our "brothers."

And yet you know that when Christ's words find a faithful heart that seeks its own good and its neighbor's, it goes right into the soul like a sword you feel you have to take up and use. "Go and correct him." The Gospel, through its commandment and advice, keeps reminding us that life is the time for action: "now is the time to act" (Ps 118: 126). It invites us not to steal, not to let our laziness and selfishness get in the way between those good ideas we have carefully worked out and formed into resolutions, and the action of putting them into practice.

Maybe this commandment of Christ's will disconcert some people—because of that refined and sometimes excessive sensitivity to the freedom and dignity of our fellows which the spirit of our times has helped develop in the consciences of Christians. For, in instructing us to give fraternal correction, our Lord is commanding us to *correct* others: that is to say, to tell someone face to face about something he is doing and ought not to be doing. And not to say it like someone who has to do a disagreeable job and cloaks it with some pleasant remark to indicate that he is really "not involved" and does it in such a way that it is as if he were apologizing and almost asking to be pitied. No; correction has to be made with a sense of personal responsibility. You have to act on your own responsibility, and you must also accept any disagreeable consequence that might result from the correction, both for yourself and for the other person. So, if we fulfill this commandment, it means going much farther than the worldly level of social convention and even friendship based on purely human standards.

Of course (because this would mean that we would not even have reached the civilized level but would be well below it) correction is not a matter of weighing into someone with ill-chosen words because, for example, he has done or said something that has annoyed us or has simply damaged "our interests" or our "good name." Obviously that's not what correction is about: that's just a way to develop resentfulness, justify revenge, and sin against charity, to a greater or lesser degree.

A person who practices the commandment of fraternal correction in a genuine Christian way is not thinking of himself but of the other person, whom he sees at that moment as a brother. He is not thinking of his self-interest or of his own reputation but of the genuine interest and reputation of the other person. He has set aside a number of considerations, especially his self-love. He has stopped thinking about himself so he can be completely concerned about the other person and about the length that person has to travel to be closely united to our Lord. If we could see the soul of that man who, taking Christ at his word, fulfills his duty to make fraternal correction, we would be completely won over by the grandeur and harmony of the sentiments that fill his heart at that moment when he gets ready to fulfill the sweet commandment of fraternal charity. We would see there a strong, refined charity, a fine, deep friendship, which is not afraid of duty, and Christian fortitude, which is a solid, cardinal virtue.

The duty to make fraternal correction reminds us that the fear of displeasing other people is not always a good thing. Unfortunately, many people, in order not to be unpleasant or to avoid telling someone that these are his last days, last hours, on earth—for example, to avoid telling someone how sick he is and thus do him very, very serious harm. But there are very many more people who see their friends' mistakes or know they are in a state of sin or are about to make a mistake or commit a sin and who don't open their mouth or move a finger to prevent this from happening.

Can we really call people who act like that our friends? Of course not. And yet they act like that because they don't want to displease us. This desire "not to displease people" can involve our friends—our neighbors—in something really evil; we can become guilty of grave sins by being, effectively, accomplices. Not to mention the fact that often, when we "dispense" ourselves from correcting others—our friends—on the grounds that they would be annoyed to receive sincere advice, given in a refined and upright way, we form opinions about them that do not do them justice—and that's not a Christian way of acting.

The duty to make fraternal correction has to be performed in a particular way. Our Lord tells us, "Go and correct him," but he goes on to say we should do it "privately." This is very interesting, this invitation to refinement, tact, and friendship. It reminds us of many Christian virtues—particularly charity, which is what moves us to speak, the virtue that looses or stops our tongue, depending on the circumstances; and then Christian prudence, which has been rightly called "the board of directors" of charity; humility, which perhaps more than any other virtue shows us how to find the right word and the right way to go about correcting someone so one doesn't offend him; fortitude and honesty, virtues that help us recognize a true man and a genuine Christian. "Privately": fraternal correction is a good secret, a proof of sincere friendship, an assurance of fidelity and loyalty.

Speaking is one thing, speaking behind a person's back is something else. Backbiting, speaking about someone to others, or telling them about something we think he has done wrong: that is a lack of charity and, often, a lack of justice. However, if you point out to the person himself what he has done wrong, if you advise your brother in a refined way, to help him correct himself, then you are obeying our Lord's commandment and doing an act of charity and showing real, Christian friendship. When we are on the point of talking about someone behind his back, let us try, with God's grace, to bring the matter to his own attention—if it is really worth mentioning—obeying at the same time those rules which should always govern the morality of our actions.

But the duty to *speak* is paralleled, naturally, by the duty to *listen*. A person who does not listen is voluntarily depriving himself of this help; he is passing up a right that is his—the right, based on charity, to receive advice, to be corrected, the right to receive effective help. What a pity it is not to listen and to be known by everyone as someone to whom nothing can be said, to be known as a Christian—in name only!—who proudly rejects any help from others. Self-love separates and sets us apart from others; it condemns us to solitary existence. It reduces us to that tragic condition which the Scriptures deplore: "Woe to him who is alone, for when he falls down he has no one to help him up!" (Ecclesiastes 4: 10).

That is why our Lord says, after laying down fraternal correction as an obligation, "If he listens to you, you have won back your brother." It's true; if you listen in these circumstances, a lively Christian friendship springs up, or it is strengthened and deepened if it was already there. When we listen to advice and accept it and are grateful for it, the natural bond of friendship is raised to the level of Christian friendship. Winning and being won by others in this way means feeling the breath of the spirit of the Gospel in our relationships and friendships.

If we listen to others when they come to us with this evangelical approach, in this charitable way, we are practicing, especially, the virtue of humility, for no other virtue better disposes us to knowing the truth and receiving peace into our hearts. And truth and peace will make it much easier for us, with God's help, to go in the right direction and smooth the road of our moral life. These interior dispositions very quickly produce an attitude of real gratitude toward that brother of ours who is taking our problems and well-being so much to heart; our friendship with him will grow stronger, out of loyal sincerity and heartfelt gratitude.

Let us, therefore, add another one to the list of those questions we ask ourselves in our daily examination of conscience—about doing our duty to make fraternal correction. And in order to make all our friendships ever more genuine and Christian, let's protect them by fulfilling this sweet commandment of our Lord.

THE DANGER OF GOOD THINGS

The supernatural good of any one person is better than the natural good of the entire universe (Summa Theologiae, I, II, q. 113, a. 9 ad 2). *We should ask God always to keep this belief and this supernatural outlook before our minds—to give us this objective hierarchy in our ideas and affections and actions. We need to ask God to give us this approach, for*
it is a gift of God.

JOSEMARÍA ESCRIVÁ DE BALAGUER, MARCH 24, 1931

THE MASSES for the Sundays after Pentecost often contain passages from Saint Luke's Gospel. One of them invites us to meditate on the parable of the great banquet (Lk 14: 15ff.). It is nice to hear Jesus speak about meals and invitations and guests. . . . These are familiar things, and their very ordinariness leads us to draw near, in simplicity of soul, with a desire to understand his meaning better.

Let us try—as we have been doing all through these pages—to make as transparent as possible the veil that, as in every one of our Lord's parables, is drawn over its simple, deep beauty. Words of Christ on the very same page of the Gospel seem to encourage us to do this: "Listen, anyone who has ears to hear." They invite us to make an effort, really to bend our mind and heart to listen to what he is saying. But at the same time they are a kind of warning: for souls who are spiritually sensitive, these words of our Lord contain a kind of challenge. They involve risk—the risk of having to face up to certain spiritual and apostolic undertakings in the future, the risk of having to live a more productive and, in the last analysis, more joyful and serene life.

The great banquet—in that passage from Saint Luke—is Christ's redemption, the infinite merits of Christ our Lord. It is a "great" banquet because "in him generous redemption is to be found" (Ps 129: 7). With those gentle, pressing invitations that he sent out, he invited a large number of people: these are calls he addresses to each and every man, asking him to share in the effects of the Redemption and to live in such a way that the infinite merits of the Redeemer are applied to him. It is a banquet prepared for us—for you and me. If we are sincere about it, the infinite merits of Christ will be ours; each of us can look at the Redeemer and say after Saint Paul: "He loved me and gave himself up for me" (Gal 2: 20).

It is reassuring to see from the parable that, to avoid making us feel forced (for if the invitation had come from a king, one might have felt under an obligation to attend), the Lord describes himself in a general sort of way; rather than make you feel shy, he invites you to intimacy and friendship; he calls himself simply "a man"—it could be anyone, it could be any one of us. And indeed we are being invited by one who calls himself *Filius hominis:* the Son of man—by the Son of God become man; by him who, out of love for us men, "emptied himself, taking the form of a servant" (Phil 12: 7).

When we understand this meaning of the parable, we do of course want to listen to the invitation being issued to us all to "come along"; and our heart is filled with confidence when we see that the host has everything ready. That makes it very easy for us to accept the invitation and set out, aided by his strength and his grace.

Yet we are quite surprised when we hear the replies to the invitations; everyone who has been invited declines, although in a very nice way: "Please accept my apologies." But if we stop to examine the excuses they give for not going, we are also inclined to admit that they seem to be very sensible. The first man has a very good excuse: "I have bought a piece of land and must go and see it." And the second excuse is almost as good: "I have bought five yoke of oxen and am on my way to try them out." And, of course, the third man seems to have the best excuse of all: "I have just married and so am unable to go."

Perhaps it is here that the veil of the parable is least transparent: for after secretly sympathizing with the people who decline the invitations—because they seem to have very good excuses—we then see the anger of the father of the family and hear his severe condemnation of those who declined: "I tell you, not one of those who were invited shall have a taste of my banquet." Perhaps for a brief moment we are caught off guard and are tempted to see a certain disproportion between the guests' refusals—on apparently valid grounds, and given in a very mannerly way—and the anger and severity of the man who invited them.

However, we will cease to be surprised and the veil will again become transparent as soon as we recognize that the great banquet is the eternal salvation of each man, of each of the invitees. Our eternal salvation really is a tall order: just think of the damage done to us by original sin, which so easily leads us to use good things in bad ways.

Christ's parable invites us to think along these lines: the excuses offered by those invited are genuine excuses (in other words, they are not telling lies); when declining the invitation, they do so in a pleasant, well-mannered way; the things that take up their time are good things. And yet it is true that they are neglecting the most important thing in order to do less important things; it is still true they have compromised and have rashly put at risk their eternal salvation, which is represented in the parable as the great banquet. And that is precisely what the parable is trying to denounce—the danger that lies in all good things when we get so caught up in them that we go farther and farther away from God; the danger that good things, when not used in the right way, at the right time, and to the right degree, will lead us to give up our duties of piety and our apostolic commitments, thus endangering the union of our souls with God and, as time goes by, maybe losing completely any sense of God.

It has been said, quite truly to my mind, that many work in politics, the arts, industry, or business but that very few really work at their own sanctification, at the salvation of their own soul, at the great business of their eternal sanctification. You know very well that, in themselves, these activities—politics, culture, business—are not something bad; in fact they can be good, very good indeed. It is man who, sometimes, does not know how to engage in them so as to make them useful to his salvation and lead him to his last end: like those who decline the invitation, he is a victim of good things. One of those carried away by temporal things and by good works cried disconsolately: "Selflessness has been the ruin of me!" That should put us on our guard.

We, all of us, continually feel harassed by this simple temptation (so easy to yield to, so difficult to shake off)—the temptation to relegate to the very last place the duties of our Christian life, and to attend to them when we have "time" and when we "feel like it." We approach the matter in a very shallow and scarcely supernatural sort of way; we give in very easily, and we end up regarding those duties that have to do with our last end as simply "one more thing" and not as absolute duties of state (duties that are a direct result of our being Christians) and as the most important thing in life. And that is very, very silly and very imprudent: but our mind, light-headed and superficial, calculates frantically and elaborates complicated arguments, which don't take into account eternity and the salvation of our soul. The great warnings in the Gospel ("Only one thing is necessary. . ."; "What does it profit a man . . . ?"; "Be watchful. . ."; etc.) carry little or no weight when we have to make decisions or in the way we approach our problems.

But if our mind doesn't work very well, neither does our will, and the superficiality of our judgments is reflected also in the inconsistencies in our Christian life—in our omissions and negligence. Every Christian ought to reflect carefully, every night, on things pertaining to his last end that he has omitted or neglected during the day—not to get depressed about it but to help recover lost ground. Anyone who, like us, is bent on living life to the full ought every day to get around to all his duties, as our Lord himself suggested (". . . these you ought to have done, without neglecting others"—Mt 23: 23), to make sure that none of them is neglected or postponed without cause.

We need, above all, that serene, balanced Christian way of judging things; a judgment that, by being open to eternity and keeping our last end in view, enables us to measure everything properly; and we need an upright, decisive will acting on that judgment and able to avoid any omission and generously make up for any negligence.

This and no other is the road we should travel if we are to steer our way through temporal goods and use them properly, never losing sight of eternal goods. And that is what the Church often prays for in the time after Pentecost. It is a prayer we too ought address to our Lord, entrusting it to her who is the Mediatrix of all graces.

THE WEEDS AND THE GOOD WHEAT

The parables are a divine teaching method—bright and clear to simple souls; unintelligible to those who are complicated and indocile: that is why the Pharisees do not understand them. The sower, the field, the enemy, the cockle . . . Go nearer Christ, and tell him to explain the parable to you —edissere nobis parabolam—in the intimacy of your prayer.

JOSEMARÍA ESCRIVÁ DE BALAGUER, MARCH 24, 1931

THESE DAYS I have reread the parable of the weeds in the field, and some words of our Lord made a particular impression on me: "When the plants came up and bore grain, the weeds appeared as well" (Mt 13: 26). A good man had sown good seed in his field, and then his enemy came under cover of darkness and sowed weeds among it.

In our meditation in the presence of the Lord, we will stop at these few words I have just quoted. We will stop to consider these weeds that grow up among good wheat, and go on to consider how, in our soul, evil sprouts up also on top of good and along with good. Those few words invite us to be attentive, to be watchful, to make sure that we don't turn into evil the good there is in us, the good we have achieved or are achieving, and that we don't fail to pursue good because of incidental evil.

The words of Jesus speak of something of which we have intimate and personal experience. In our soul and in our life, as in the field in the parable, evil sprouts up on top of and alongside good. And we have to strive tenaciously and to be vigilant to ensure that good is not destroyed, reduced, or corrupted. With the help of ascetical doctrine, let us explore our personal experience—the experience of Christians who want to live in a Christian way—so we can see how the painful story of the parable is repeated in our lives.

Here, to begin with, is a first example taken from the Gospel. Two men went up to the temple to pray: here is good wheat, here is something very good—prayer, adoration the creature renders his Creator, conversation of the son with his Father. But we find that, in the prayer of one of these two men, the evil of pride sprouts up, the evil of self-satisfaction, even to the extent of despising the other man: on top of and along with good, therefore, evil sprouts up. The Pharisee stood there and said this prayer to himself: "I thank you, God, that I am not like the rest of men" (Lk 18: 11). In the sphere of virtue, it is not uncommon, unfortunately, to find that amid the (great and beautiful) good of chastity, there sometimes grows up the evil of pride and contempt for others. Nor is it rare—our personal experience may give us proof of this—to see raising its head the same evil of contempt for others in the field of a life of honesty and sacrifice.

There is no doubt that fasting is something good, even a great good—nowadays, unfortunately, a little neglected. The word of God reminds us: "Prayer is good when it is accompanied by fasting . . ." (Tob 12: 8). And yet our Lord advises us to be watchful, to ensure that in the midst of the good of sacrifice the evil of vanity does not rear its head; that would undermine all that good, because the vain man will receive no reward other than the ridiculous one (if he receives even that) of the human applause he so foolishly seeks. To avoid that evil growing up among that particular good, our Lord warns us, "When you fast, wash your face and anoint your head" (Mt 6: 16), which is like saying: Watch to make sure your intention is right so that the good you do is not undermined and destroyed by the evil of vanity.

This weed is the same kind as that which encroaches on the gifts of nature and grace and the good things we achieve by means of those gifts—when we complacently make out they are our own property and fail to acknowledge that God has given them to us.

To avert danger of this weed, the Apostle of the Gentiles puts a blunt question to us: "What have you that you have not received?" (1 Cor 4: 7).

We all know that, in the supernatural field, there is nothing greater than charity. And yet even on that queen of virtues, evil is getting ready to plant its germ. Charity, if it is to continue to be genuine charity, has to be ordered. The hierarchy of charity is first of all to love God above all things; then to love people—our neighbor—in an ordered way, according to his nearness to

God, on the one hand, and to ourselves, on the other. Inverting that hierarchy and order means not loving in a correct and Christian way: it means that the evil of selfishness has grown over the good of charity. Loving other people means wishing them well, that is to say, desiring their good, which is supernatural good. On this point it is common enough to see weeds growing among Christians' charity: they think they love when they give the people they say they love (and by whom they want to be loved) goods that are not truly good, for those goods are opposed to their genuine good. How many times people try to pass off as love something that isn't love at all, but pure selfishness and sometimes refined selfishness! When that happens, we are not loving other people for God and for their own sake, but only for our sake. The evil of selfishness keeps on growing over the good of charity, undermining it and destroying it.

No one can doubt that the apostolate, activity carried out for the good of souls, is something very valuable. But if that activity, however good and holy it is, makes us do without prayer or neglect our life of piety or forget our duties of state, then sooner or later it will turn into weeds, into cockle, which crops up precisely in the middle of the good wheat of Christ. When in the previous chapter we were speaking about the "danger of good things," we heard the anguished lament of a soul who spotted too late the weeds sown among his good seed, and who on seeing the field of his soul sown with these weeds, exclaimed: "Selflessness has been the ruin of me." To warn us against this danger we have those words of Christ to the sister of Mary of Bethany: "Martha, you worry and fret about so many things, but only one thing is necessary" (Lk 10: 4). But also in another case, when love for souls, zeal for their good, ceases to be refined and becomes uncouth or bitter, we are witnessing the growth of evil among good, weeds sprouting up among the good wheat. In this connection we can remember what our Lord said to control the impatience of those two disciples who were called the "sons of thunder" and who wanted to bring fire down from heaven to punish the inhabitants of a city whose occupants had not immediately accepted the Good News when it was preached to them; he rebuked them, saying, "You do not know the spirit in which you share." For sometimes what happens is that at first we do not fulfill our duty, and then, hardened by a spirit of atonement and by a fervor that goes too far, we want to do more than our duty entails. The same teaching can, I think, be deduced from the parable of the weeds: the laborers at first fail in their duty by falling asleep and then want to do too much, rooting out the weeds before time. But the owner of the field is prudent and moderate: "Let them both grow until harvest time."

And so it is that evil can often crop up amid goodness (if men are not really watchful). Love for truth and goodness can, unfortunately, turn into fanaticism and a caste attitude when (because one is not properly enlightened, or one is not very charitably disposed toward others) we fail in practice to distinguish between sin and the sinner, between error and those who err. And it can also happen that, once people have started down this slippery slope, even though they are dedicated to good, they act as if good is not really good unless done by themselves.

It is certainly true that "spirituality" is a good thing, even the best of things. But if a man forgets that he is not only spirit but also matter, if he thinks he is an angel, he will not be long in turning into a rebellious angel, a result of that pride which has taken him out of his true place. Then the consequences are tragic: "I saw Satan fall like lightning from heaven" (Lk 10: 18). Those who proudly put themselves on a pedestal that could never be theirs have such a mighty fall that it reminds you of the first rebellious angel. How many examples there are of this in the history of mankind! Yet we never manage to learn the lesson.

There is no need to recall how holy and necessary it is for one's own sanctification and for the attainment of the common good, for subjects to have respect and reverence for their superiors; but if this holy and proper respect turns into servility, then the goodness has gone. Something bad has sprouted up, something that in fact prevents subjects from serving their superiors in an upright way. Servility destroys the relationship of subordination because it deprives the subject of loyalty and sincerity. It undermines his human dignity; it hinders him from rendering genuine and upright service. The same thing happens with obedience when it is wrongly understood: it can suppress the spirit of initiative and of personal responsibility, turning it into laziness and love of comfort. Here again are evils that grow up in and around goodness. It is a repetition of the parable of the weeds, taking place in the intimacy of our souls and in our ordinary life. And the same thing happens when, through proud impatience at the human defects on the face of the spouse of Christ, love for the Church is turned into pharisaical scandal, which cannot grasp the mystery of the Church. The good sons of the Church (those for whom the Church is *Sancta Mater Ecclesia*) never try to edge out God's wisdom to make room for their personal viewpoints; and so, by adoring God's plan, they are able to grasp the mystery of the Church as far as it is humanly possible to do so.

We could continue with more examples, but we have said enough to help us understand that this parable refers very directly to our soul: evil often arises amid goodness, just as the weeds sprout up among the good seed. And to finish, let us take from the parable two pieces of advice, to help us avoid evil drowning goodness in our soul and in our lives. The first is that invitation of our Lord to be vigilant so as to avoid what caused all the evil in the parable: ". . . while men slept. . . ." Sleep, inattentiveness, and negligence favor the action of the enemy and the growth of evil, all the more so because the enemy *does not sleep*; on the contrary, the more good a man does, the more the enemy tempts him and lies in wait for him. The Scriptures warn us: "Let the man who is standing be careful he does not fall." The second piece of advice that Christ offers us refers to patience, patience with ourselves and with others: "In patience, by endurance, you will possess your souls." The Gospel tells us somewhere else: the ultimate price of our holiness is, then, patience—the perseverance that lets the word of God yield a harvest (cf. Lk 8: 15). Patience, which is always humble; and prudence; and a humble will—which make sure we never substitute our own plans for God's plans.

LIGHT FROM BETHLEHEM

This is how God goes about doing things: one thing after another,
guiding our steps, using secondary causes, using people as his instruments.

JOSEMARÍA ESCRIVÁ DE BALAGUER, JANUARY 25, 1961

ALL THE MYSTERIES of Christ's life are mysteries of love; the very birth of the Son of God is a mystery of love. Only divine omnipotence placed at the service of an infinite love for men could have found such a wonderful way of fulfilling the ancient promise. The event can be explained only by reference to him who caused it: these are words the Church gives her priests to say about the mystery that takes place in the cave at Bethlehem.

This mystery of God's becoming a child really is a mystery of love: he who is all-powerful reduces himself to complete powerlessness. The Lord of heaven and earth has not even a cradle to lie in; a stable acts as a palace for the Son of David; a manger is used as a throne for the Son of God.

Today, as we wonder at the mystery of God's having become a child, let us try to make a real effort to understand the value and importance of a genuine life of spiritual childhood. In his public life, to show us the only route he could guarantee would bring us to the kingdom, he said: "Unless you become like little children, you will never enter the kingdom of heaven" (Mt 18: 3). That is all we have to pay to attend the "show" in heaven, to enjoy God's glory and beauty and harmony. And it is a price outside the reach of proud people and very much within the reach of the humble and of all those who, by making an effort, become men of goodwill.

Surely all of us, this Christmas night, feel the need to try to sanctify ourselves, to become like little children, as this child–God wants? Particularly if we are in today's world, where it is so easy to grow old and even die spiritually while still being young in years and apparently fresh and healthy.

How many young people and adults do we not know who are spiritually dead! How many complicated, closed people whose souls are like labyrinths and whose hearts are always in commotion!

Christmas is the time for simplicity, for being born again, and for spiritual childhood. We should grasp this opportunity, when Christ comes to children and speaks to them. A simple, pure glance will be enough to go deeper into this mystery and enjoy it and benefit from it.

The greatest event in the history of mankind took place in the simplest of ways; something totally supernatural happened in the most natural of ways. The edict of a pagan emperor, Caesar Augustus, brought Mary and Joseph to Bethlehem; and they were spared none of the harshness of a long, difficult journey, in which cold and privation were their only companions.

God's action in the world and the work of divine providence in the government of human life pass unnoticed by men and by the chroniclers of history, when people who ought to see and appreciate and report these events fail to approach them with a simple heart, which alone lets them be party to secrets of the life of faith. We men have become so used to looking for noisy news, we are so keen on spectacular events, that we fail to understand God's preference for simple, ordinary things. There must have been hundreds of other ways of bringing Mary and Joseph to Bethlehem; but divine providence, using a very simple and ordinary way, chose one that certainly was not the most comfortable way for Joseph and Mary, "his betrothed, who was with child" (Lk 2: 5). There is a lesson here for us in the twentieth century, who are always looking for the extraordinary, the unusual, who are forever looking for new ways to have an easy life.

The journey that Mary and Joseph made to Bethlehem is simple, humble, and spectacular. And the same can be said of the birth of the very Son of God: it takes place in the humility and poverty of a cave, in the middle of a cold, silent night.

It certainly cannot be said that silence and solitude are *our* popular constant companions. In our normal day, periods of silence are few and far between. We hardly know what it means to fight against noise in our soul. And solitude, more than anything else—let's be frank about it—makes us afraid; we often associate it with boredom and tedium.

In the birth of the Son of God, poverty is so complete that it takes on a certain grandeur—and it is so simple that it borders on poetry. He who adorns the flowers, the fields, and the birds has hardly the wherewithal to cover his nakedness. Many doors have been closed to him; many others have not opened to him: the two wayfarers have sought in vain a roof to shelter them for the night. "There was no room for them in the inn."

A cave, a manger, a handful of straw, two farm animals—a donkey and a cow. This is the time and place chosen by Providence to start the Christian era. And, while they stayed there, the time came for the mother to deliver her child, the time of the great promise: and she gave birth to her firstborn son and wrapped him in swaddling clothes and laid him in a manger. The scene is complete: Mary, the Mother of God; Joseph, the supposed father of Jesus; and the newly-born King of the Jews lying in the manger. All very simple, all very poor. A poor mother, a just man, simple swaddling clothes, a little child, a stable, a manger. We are in the middle of winter and in the middle of the night.

When we contemplate all this poverty and remember that the baby is the Light of the world, we naturally ask ourselves whether we have not ignored up to now—or at least not grasped sufficiently—how necessary the virtue of poverty is for our Christian life: without this virtue we cannot enter the kingdom of heaven.

It's very sad that so many people disregard this virtue altogether and live so wastefully and frivolously. This desire for the superfluous, for *more, more* temporal possessions, unfortunately dictates the manner of their living and gives the true measure of very many people: it seems that the light of Bethlehem has not reached them. And very few seem to have taken to heart our Lord's commandment: "Give what is left over to the poor" (Lk 11: 41). The borderline between what is necessary and what is superfluous is continually shifting in the outlook and aims and lives of many Christians. And to the extent that it is pushed back, they lose serenity and joy. They are constantly creating new needs; they want to acquire and enjoy more and more things. And no sooner do you get them and enjoy them than, infallibly, you become disillusioned with them and your heart becomes dry again and your hands empty. But off you go again, immediately, in the same direction, with the same objectives.

If we stay for a while at the cave of Bethlehem, we will learn about the virtue of detachment—which means wanting to be poor and, insofar as is possible, becoming really poor—and we can savor the blessedness of poverty: "Blessed are the poor of spirit, for theirs is the kingdom of heaven." A heart detached from the things of this world floods the soul with peace and teaches it to put to good use any wealth it possesses, thereby developing the virtue of generosity. Moreover, detachment gives serenity of heart, which is perfect interior freedom.

If we now look away from the crib, to the nearby hills, the shepherds will win us over by their simplicity. They are simple, humble, and poor. There they are, doing their duty, keeping guard over their flocks. That is why they are the first to be told the Good News; that is why they become the first to adore the Son of God. The choices God makes are always conditioned by the presence in souls of those virtues that give off a genuinely evangelical perfume. The darkness opens up, the silence of the night is broken, and the angel brings the shepherds the joy of the Good News. "I bring you news of great joy. . . ." Our simplicity will decide how much we share in the joy of the birth of Christ. The angels, while praising God, promise peace—the peace of the Christ who has been born—to men of goodwill. Men of goodwill! That's the true "class" to which all Christians should belong. If we all had this evangelical "goodwill," social classes, even if they continued to exist, would cease contending with each other, and we would attain, all together, the *pax Christi in regno Christi:* the peace of Christ in the kingdom of Christ.

Let us correct our will, here in front of the cave of Bethlehem, and make it really "good," ready faithfully to serve the Lord. For if we manage, with the help of the light from Bethlehem, to become simple souls and men of goodwill, we will deeply share in the greatness of this day "on which appeared the goodness and loving kindness of God our Savior" (Tit 3: 4). May the Virgin of Bethlehem, the Mother of Christ, teach us how to become renewed "on the inside" and to understand and enjoy the goodness and kindness of our Savior, the Christ who has been born.